This is not simply a book for alcoholics; it's a book for anyone who has dealt with pain and been left scrabbling after God. Raw, sobering, miraculously ordinary, hopeful, beautiful, and yet terrifying.

—SARAH BESSEY, author of *Out of Sorts*

We've all got our vices, but without them, how would we cope? Along comes Haines, with a luminous pen, an uncommon authenticity, and a palpable hope for anyone who's tired of numbing the pain.

—JENNIFER DUKES LEE, author of *Love Idol*

Haines' honesty is refreshing, his faith is challenging, his hope is encouraging, his love is passionate, and his portrait of God's grace is amazing.

—GLENN R. KREIDER, Dallas Theological Seminary

Within these pages I not only became engrossed in the beauty and pain of Haines' journey, but I also found bits of my own humanity. One of the best books about faith I've read this year.

—MATTHEW PAUL TURNER, author of *Churched*

I honestly don't know how to put into words how this book has opened my eyes, healed me, pushed me, and brought me peace. But it has done all those things, and I will never be the same.

—ANNIE F. DOWNS, author of *Let's All Be Brave*

Haines commands language and style so deftly the work reads like the highest literary fiction. Approachable and witty, this is a sobering reflection, no matter your addiction.

—PRESTON YANCEY, Anglican Diocese of the Western Gulf Coast

A profoundly courageous work that provides a major dose of hope and guidance, whether or not you struggle with the more conventional addictions. You will be encouraged and inspired.

—REV. MIHEE KIM-KORT, author of *Making Paper Cranes*

With honest pain and discovery dappled with poetry, Haines prophesies to us of what it means to find the peace of God and the forgiveness of Christ. Read these words; you will never be the same.

—ZACH J. HOAG, author, preacher, and blogger

Haines had me imagining what the world could look like if we all were widening our wounds, bleeding together, rejoicing in the astounding, transformative work of suffering, and coming clean as a global community.

—ERIKA MORRISON, author of *Bandersnatch*

If honesty were an ocean, Haines boldly goes to the depths. Hopefully, this book will not only teach us to swim; it will teach us to start diving.

—A. J. SWOBODA, PhD, pastor, author, professor

Coming Clean is a gift of redemptive lyric, growing out of sober reflection that quietly compels the reader to honestly process their own faith journey.

—THOMAS ADDINGTON, PhD, cofounder and CEO, Givington's

Raw and soothing by turns, this memoir is a fine creation, one that provides a plumb line for anyone who has walked away from the simple center of faith.

—JAMIE A. HUGHES, award-winning editor and writer

Haines' honest words invite us all to come clean before a God who is comfortable in the mess. This is a book of uncommon depth and beauty.

—JAMIN GOGGIN, author of *Beloved Dust*

This is a book about about coming clean, yes, but also about faith and pain and how we try to medicate our fear that nobody is listening when we pray. Haines' honest words give me hope.

—MICAH J. MURRAY, blogger at *micahjmurray.com*

Haines forces us to look at the realities of our own pain, but shows us the way of healing by directing us to the goodness of God. I've waited my whole life for this book.

—NISH WEISETH, author of *Speak*

COMING CLEAN

COMING CLEAN
A Story of Faith

SETH HAINES

ZONDERVAN®

ZONDERVAN

Coming Clean
Copyright © 2015 by Seth Haines

This title is also available as a Zondervan ebook. Visit www.zondervan.com/ebooks.

Requests for information should be addressed to:
Zondervan, 3900 *Sparks Dr. SE, Grand Rapids, Michigan 49546*

Published in association with William K. Jensen Literary Agency, 119 Bampton Court, Eugene, Oregon 97404.

Cover design: Dual Identity
Cover photography: © Picsfive/Shutterstock®
Interior design: Kait Lamphere

First printing August 2015 / Printed in the United States of America

To Amber: you are every reason.

To my sons: this fire alarm is for you. Break
glass and pull in case of emergency.

To my grandchildren: see the above instructions to your fathers.

To inner sobriety: you have taught me to hear the Spirit.

To the Spirit: you have led me in the paths
of inner sobriety; you are the Muse.

CONTENTS

FOREWORD

This is a book about alcohol; you can practically smell the gin coming off the pages, the lime, hear the ice clinking, the crack of the new bottle opening. But it's not a book about alcohol. It's about whatever thing you use to cover over the pain—sex, food, shopping, perfectionism, cleaning, drugs—whatever you hold out like an armor to protect yourself instead of allowing yourself and your broken heart to be fully seen and fully tended to by God.

For me, the armor is motion. Activity. Busyness. More, more, more. Faster, faster, faster. If I can keep going fast enough, I can, for a little while at least, outrun the fear and the anxiety and the pain. And so I go and go and go, working and writing and grocery shopping, cooking and reading and folding laundry. Silence is my enemy.

But I'm learning to walk into the arms of that enemy. And to my great surprise, I'm finding a friend there, not an enemy at all. I'm finding a healer—the Healer. The Good Physician, the Great Friend. And when I walk toward him, I can lay down my addictions for a while. I can lay down my frantic running. I can rest, and that feeling is utterly transformational.

We all have those armors. Some we've chosen; some have been handed down through the generations. About my propensity toward constant motion, my husband reminds me lovingly that I come by it honestly. I'm my father's daughter in a thousand ways, many of them good. And also this one: we're both bent on outrunning things. We're both good at it.

And now that he is sixty-three and I am thirty-eight, we're getting good at another thing: reminding one another to put on the brakes. At Christmas last year, we were away—my mom and dad, my brother, my husband, our boys. My dad waited for the right moment, several days into the trip. We looked out at the water together, and he told me my engines were running too hot. I was burning people, burning myself out.

It takes one to know one. And he was right. The tears rolled down my face because I knew he was right. And so I began again, toward sobriety, toward silence, toward that inner emptiness that I always think can be filled up with endless activity.

This beautiful, challenging, evocative book is an invitation toward the deepest kind of sobriety: the kind that lays us bare to Christ, which is the only place where the wounds we've suffered— many at our own hand—can finally be healed. And along the way, we find that the scars become holy places, reminders of the Healer himself.

Seth writes with a distinctly southern sensibility—elegant, evocative, lyrical—and his wisdom and honesty shine through every page, gently illuminating our own fears and secret hearts along the way.

—SHAUNA NIEQUIST, AUTHOR OF
BREAD AND WINE AND SAVOR

SHALL WE BEGIN HERE?
An Open Invitation

In the late summer, some years ago, I woke one morning to a lavish Christian hangover.

This is the truest way I know to begin this exposition of coming clean, and though it's still difficult to accept the moniker alcoholic, I know that I am, in the most colloquial sense, dependent. Yes, I am an enjoyable, joyous, exuberant dependent.

I have found that at my most drunk, I am also my most fun. This would be the second truest way I know to begin this exposition of my coming clean. When the numbing of the liquor set in, when it deadened fiery anxiety and inhibitions, a permanent smile washed over me, and the clever, quippy comments rained. I felt less angst; I felt the dissipation of life's groaning.

In this age of Christian liberty, of the disentanglement of the Christian ethos and prohibition, I found myself stretching deeper and deeper into the bottle in an effort to avoid pain. I found myself dependent upon something other than the God in which I professed faith.

Why? We'll get to that.

For now, though, know this: this is a journaling of my days of coming clean. It is not a book as one normally thinks of a book. Perhaps you'll find a narrative arc. Perhaps you won't. What you'll find, I hope, is an honest piece of writing that tracks my first ninety days of sobriety, one that deals with pain, with healing, and ultimately, with the mystery able to help us all come clean.

We'll get to that too.

Know this also: this is not a book about alcoholism or alcohol dependency. It is a book about the human experience. We've all felt the pain in this groaning and grinding of life. We all cope in different ways. Some drink, some abuse prescription drugs, some overeat, some undereat or puke or have sex or amass wealth or give all their wealth away. Some overintellectualize life, build super-structures of theological certainties so that they do not have to confront the real, abiding, fearsome, mysterious God.

We all have our vices, see.

Know this three: this is not a program; it is not the last chapter of a journey. This is the beginning—my beginning. Maybe even yours. It is the shedding of the first garment on the way to naked. This is an exposition of my process of stripping off the falsities, of coming clean.

Read this less as a book about alcoholism and more as one about the pains and salves common to every life. My alcoholism is not the thing, see. Neither is your eating disorder, your greed disorder, or your sex addiction. Your sin is not the thing. The thing is under the sin. The thing is the pain. Sin management without redemption of life's pain is a losing proposition.

There is an antidote for the pain. It was taught to us, com-manded of us, modeled for us. It is simple in word and sometimes impossible in deed. It is free, but it isn't cheap.

Are you ready to explore with me? Are you ready to find the medicine?

This is an open invitation to come clean.

PART 1
THE SEEING

I am tangled up in contradictions. I am strangled by my own two hands. I am hunted by the hounds of addiction. Hosanna!

—ANDREW PETERSON, "HOSANNA"

SEPTEMBER 26

Once, I was a hopeful man. Once, I spouted verses in the cloying language that belongs to all clichés. "All things work together for good," I said, and for the most part, they always had. Once, I believed my career—as an attorney for the largest firm in the grand state of Arkansas—would be a shining success, my marriage a model of fidelity, my four boys—Isaac, Jude, Ian, and Titus—the strapping sort of Ozark woodsmen who could fell mighty oaks with a single axe swoop.

Amber and I were church pillars in those days, the kind who led home groups in our spacious farmhouse hewn of 1938 Ozark stone. On the weekends, we sat in our deep couch, swirling glasses of wine with younger married couples and schooling them in the art of connection. We quoted Scripture, prayed often and together. Our eldest children learned John 3:16 before the other boys in their Sunday morning class. Things were sorted, figured, and comfortable.

That was before we had Titus.

Titus was a mystery baby from the first. He was born with a hole in his heart and a rate of respiration that jogged a little faster than most. Even still, nothing could stop his smile. His brothers took turns doting on him and making eyes at his cooing joy. They lured laughs with peekaboos. Even Ian, whose baby birth order had been upset, adjusted to the new joys, loved the big-brotherness of it all.

At six months, Titus developed a large lump on the right side of his neck. The node swelled until it reached the size of a large marble. The doctors pronounced it an invasive strain of staph infection, and it seemed resistant to all but the strongest antibiotics. Weeks of treatment passed, yet as the lymph node shrank, so did Titus. First he stopped growing. Then he did what no infant is meant to do: he began losing weight.

Mild panic morphed into a full-blown medical emergency. Titus turned into a monitoring project, a newborn mystery under the careful and constant watch of our hospital's medical team. But when they could muster no answers, Titus was sent to the Arkansas Children's Hospital.

Follow me into the hospital; see my son.

Titus is just under one year old, and he is a small bag of bones. He is energetic but hollow. Some say he is thin, but I say gaunt. The doctors once labeled him acutely malnourished, and now they say that he has failed to thrive. They have assembled around him as if he is an alien. They have needled him, prodded him, and scanned him.

The specialists at Arkansas Children's Hospital tell us, "This little one is an anomaly." Everything is a little off: his brain stem sags slightly into his spinal column; his respiratory rate is elevated, but only just so; his heart beats a little fast; the minerals in his blood are just a little outside of tolerances. He is skewed a bit in almost every direction.

He is an angel, though; they all say it. His eyes are as bright as full moons, their size amplified by his bird-thin rib cage and narrow face. I count his ribs with the concern of a father, but the nurses do not notice. They play with him, gift him stuffed animals, and coax him into pulling up on the bed rails. He laughs, smiles, flirts, then pauses. He stiffens, falls to the mattress, and vomits his last feeding across the bedsheet. He splays listlessly across the bed. The nurses console him in small whispers. Amber rubs his naked back and cries. Titus has not held nourishment for a week. We fear the worst.

Oh death, where is your sting? The Scripture comes to mind, but not in the voice of comfort. Instead, it comes in a mocking tenor.

Titus is taken to another exam room, and this time, we force him to drink a viscous blue fluid. I pin his shoulders to the mattress and hold his head while the nurses force the liquid into his mouth through a syringe. They clamp his jaws shut, and he lurches and jerks until he gives in and swallows. (Oh, the terrible things we do for love.) We place him on the table, where the mechanical arm and electronic eye look past his skin and into his digestive tract. The electronic eye captures his peristalsis, and Titus, invaded by the all-seeing eye, screams and tries to kick free. I wear a lead vest and hold his arms above his head while a lead-vested nurse holds his legs straight. He is on the rack, and we are stretching him past infanthood. He thrashes, and I fear his arms and legs will bruise from our restraining him. Amber stands behind the glass, hand over her mouth and worry weighing on her brow.

Oh death, where is your sting?

The doctor comes to our room, tells us that he is sorry, but he cannot find the cause of my son's illness. "We will discharge you tomorrow and regroup," he says. "We'll hope to see you in two weeks with a new game plan." We wonder whether Titus can make it another two weeks without eating. I refuse to leave, tell the doctor that we need answers. He measures once, then cuts. "He can stay," he says, "but we're running out of options. We will do our best to make him comfortable, and I'll consult with my colleague. Perhaps he'll have some idea."

The doctor leaves the hospital room, and Amber and I begin discussing funeral songs. I consider the songs of Rich Mullins, my go-to bard. "'The Love of God'?" I ask, "'Creed'?" I feel neither in the moment.

Oh death, where is your sting?

I look at Titus's exposed ribs, and it is right there, the sting.

I pray for deliverance and freedom for my youngest son, but

my prayers sink on Peter's faith. Maybe Christ is asking me to leave the boat, to walk on the water. I look at him. "No! Come to me; come to Titus!"

In this moment, in this hospital room, I resolve to pray no more for Titus. He will be either healed or not. Either way, I will not saddle God with the burden of success or failure. I call Joseph, my friend and brother, and tell him that I cannot carry the burden. I can pray no more. "Tell the fellas," I say, speaking of our Friday-morning prayer group, "that they'll need to pull the weight of prayer from here on out. I've prayed all the prayers I know."

I hang up the phone and reach for the Nalgene bottle of gin I cajoled my sister to smuggle in. I pour it over the crushed ice from the vending machine in the hallway and drink deep. I drown the pain, drown myself in the ice-cold gin, and I do it in cold blood.

This was my first conscious barter. Trading pain for the closest vice, I slipped into a knowing numbness. Prayer seemed an impotent remedy; gin did not.

I come from a long line of southern gentlemen, and like them, I rather like a good and proper drink. Whiskey, beer, and wine— they're all fair game. As an attorney living in the South, I always have an opportunity for evening cocktails. There are happy-hour meetings with clients, charity galas with open bars, seminars with evening mixers. Drinking is bound up in both my genes and my occupation.

There's not a drink I don't like, which is, perhaps, the problem. I'm an imbiber of tequila, scotch, and vodka. Gin, though? Gin is the liquor of nostalgia; it's the water for my southern roots. Gin is the lover of lovers, the drink of fond memories, familial bonds, and adventure.

The best gin drink I ever had came on the shores of the Shire River in Malawi. I was visiting a friend, a missionary who'd made his home in Mozambique, and we were visiting a game park in the neighboring country. A soft palette of pastels hung on the horizon, where the sun was setting in full flame. The colors dripped golden, like honey onto the far plain across the river. The perfume of lavender and wild rose mixed with the sweet smell of the river's mud.

Between the river and me, in the lilac light, there were three hippos—a mother and her two young. The guide told us to hunker down so that nature's wild mother-instinct would not turn us from quiet observers to a perceived threat.

"The stump-legged hippo," said Saul, the local river tour guide, "is our teacher. If she turns, we turn. If she walks, we retreat. If she charges, we jump into the truck and speed away."

She was, Saul said, the most dangerous animal in all of Africa. But wasn't she majestic? See the pink of her back, the breadth of her brown muscled body? He whispered these questions in my ear as he passed a highball of gin and tonic over my shoulder.

The botanical bouquet of the gin lingered, mingled with nature's perfume. It was a majestic drink—yes, there is no denying the majesty—and though I did not yet know it, it was the precursor for the pinnacle of drinks.

In the dying light, we made our way to the Range Rover and drove to the thatched-roof pavilion where dinner was served. Women in long skirts came, dancing, one twirling fire. Their hair was piled high and bundled in fabrics made from the colors of the Shire sky, and their smiles were permanent, decals on dancing machines. Course after course, the women danced, their dark skin blending into the shadows under our thatched roof, white teeth reflecting the spinning fire.

As the fire-twirler continued her endless fire dance, I excused myself and met Saul at the bar. "Give me the local stuff," I said.

He warned me, "Mr. Seth, you do not want the local flavor. It comforts the heart and eases the mind, but it tastes like petrol and burns like a torch."

"Give it to me," I demanded with false gusto, and then conjured up a smile of my own and pantomimed pounding my fist against the bar.

"Double or single?" he said, laughing.

"Double," I said. "I am an American."

Saul poured the drink. It was brown-tinged Shire swill, distilled in the guts of a dried gourd, he said. This was no triple-distilled firewater from Rocky Mountain snowmelt, nor was it moonshine from the hidden stills of Appalachian artisans.

"In Malawi, do as the Malawians," I said and shot the double straight—no chaser, no cutter.

The world went tunnel vision, and I saw the beginning of all things—the end of them too. Anxiety melted, dripped into the Shire River like the honey sky. My throat, nose, ears, cheeks—all of it burned like the swirling fires of the flame-twirling dancer. I sputtered before remembering I was a man bound by space and time. I looked at the barkeep and Saul, who'd been watching the fire rising in my cheeks and up through my ears. Saul laughed, pulled his fingers from his ears on either side, and made the sound of a steaming teakettle. He hugged me, pulled me close.

"You are one of the people from the Shire now," he said with a chuckle and a slap on my back. It must be true, I thought, because I could feel the same fire burning behind my eyes that I saw reflected in his.

I was one of them.

It was the best drink, the drink that initiated me into another people. It was the kind of drink that fiery smiles and worriless nights are made of. It was 2008, the days when I drank for joy—or so I thought.

⌒

Once, I toasted all things beautiful—my marriage, good friends gathering around the table, a fine piece of poetry, the honey sky over the Shire—but the toasting of joys and the drowning of sorrows are closer kin than one might imagine.

Somewhere along the way, my affinity for gin (and whiskey and beer and wine and any old intoxicant) and comfort collided. Somewhere, my thirst for distraction from the pains and poverties of life grew into a sweltering, parching thing. There are always feelings to be numbed, anxieties to tamp down, and panic attacks to avoid. The people of the Shire knew this, and so do I. I suppose I could have turned to things eternal—didn't Jesus promise us rest?—but we seem to have a way of losing ourselves in our man-made salves—the bottle, the pill, the cheeseburger, self-inflicted starvation.

I suppose we're all drunk on something.

But not tonight. Tonight I'm writing sober for the first time. Fearful I would never write another creative sentence without the sauce, I called a friend, and she challenged me to see what words might come without the liquor. She challenged me to write through my sobriety. Perhaps ninety days' worth of clean words? And so, here I am, recording my first thoughts on the matter, and it hurts.

I quit the bottle in the wee morning hours of Saturday, September 21. How I'd love for that to be distant history, but the truth is it was only last week.

I'd slopped into my last extravagant drunk under the arms of the Spanish oak at a rented house with friends in Austin, Texas, and even as I took my last slug and fell into a cold leather couch, I didn't suppose myself to be alcohol dependent. I considered that I might wake with the dull thud that comes with having overimbibed, sure; the possibility, though, of waking to the resounding epiphany of this heavy language—*dependent*—was less than remote.

It was not my intent to be here, writing this. Tonight, I'm writing sober 535 miles from my great epiphany in Austin. I am under the influence only of full faculties. Tonight, I'm free-writing. I've needed to free-write for some time, which is to say I've needed to write from a place of freedom.

This is my first pass, a flyby attempt at recording the things that come in the newness of sobriety. In this scratching of words, I'm hoping to find creativity outside of the bottle. For so long, I've written from the gin or whiskey or wine. I have written poetry and prose and have even penned the Great American Novel—unpublished, as most Great American Novels are, of course—all under the influence. I'm afraid sobriety will mute the muse. A friend tells me this is mockery of God, that the liquor is not the muse. Another writer, a good friend who's had her own battle with the bottle, tells me her best stuff came when sobriety found her.

Maybe they're right.

This I know: the poet in me hears the melody in the juniper berries of the gin, the harmony in the tonic, and the overtones in the lime. This I also know: the poet in me would rather gussy up the poison, would rather call it anything other than what it is.

Tonight I'm writing sober for the first time. I will sleep tonight and hope to wake tomorrow with less fear and more resolve.

SEPTEMBER 27

The sleep? That didn't work—not really. It was a fitful night, the disquieting kind in which I rolled over to find Amber dead to the world at two o'clock in the morning, while I suffered this sinking feeling, this creeping notion that something is missing without the bottle. I suppose that notion will take a good while to kill, and I'm not sure I know just quite how to kill it either.

I didn't come here to write a book, so if you came here to read one, turn back now.

If you are hoping for plot, climax, and resolution, this might be a sore disappointment. After all, does life run along such a clean narrative arc? This is a diary of sorts, an exposition of a sobering mind. So, if you came here to watch all liquid courage evaporate, you've come to the right place.

As we begin, I might as well get one of the worst confessions out of the way.

Some folks come into this world with Catholic names, while others are cradle Methodists. Some are sprinkled Presbyterian, and still others are "Baptist born and Baptist bred, and when I die, I'll be Baptist dead." I wasn't born into any particular denomination, though. I only ever recall being woven into the fabric of a local church. My childhood faith was a canvas, colored and sometimes stained with charismatic, Baptist, Catholic, mystic, and evangelical theologies. I was exposed to it all and learned the rules of each. And though this rich tapestry of traditions was a blessing in so many ways, I learned one common Christian truth: there are things not normally confessed by good Christians.

We who are supposed to listen to the voice of the Holy Spirit, who are to serve as the walking image of God—we are supposed to have a different way about us. We live by supposed-tos and should-bes. Our more romantic versions of a transformed life clothed with the magic holiness of a magical God are the golden ideal. Our lives are part of the world redeemed by God and for God. Our social interactions are to reflect God; our art is to reflect God.

Right?

So as a writer of faith, a southern-born boy who calls Arkansas home, when I write of a southern morning, I'm supposed to point always to the hospitable, genteel God who created the glories of the Ozarks by his word. I give you a fog that hangs over the White River, one that draws allusions to the Spirit who clung to the deep nothing before light exploded. I'm supposed to paint one million metaphors of rebirth. What's more, I'm supposed to apply them to my life: see how the trout leaps heavenward from the tailwaters, how it gulps great breaths of another world, returns to its home where it finds strength to swim against the current?

I'm supposed to both draw strength from and give strength to these metaphors, to leave the impression that we're all walking in a larger, ordained narrative. I'm supposed to write in spiritual certainties about the mysteries of the cosmos; there is a reason for Titus's mystery ailments, isn't there?

Here's what I'm not supposed to say: sometimes I do not see an active God in the world around me. Sometimes the realities of the world are not ideal; sometimes nature's contours are not so supple. Sometimes there are no good metaphors. In the last year, I've hoped to see God active, even struggled to write it as if it were true. Instead, I have the dreadful feeling that God set all things in motion and then walked away.

Too many mornings, I wake with the dull thud. This may or may not be the day the Lord has made, if you ask me, but either way we're not exactly on speaking terms. The mist is not holy over the deep these days. There is only smog, and it is void, the cold anxiety of dead winter.

Some mornings, I am wakened by the slamming of my neighbor's car door, and peek out the window to see his taillights speeding smaller down the street. I imagine his life, how he is always chasing the next thing—the promotion, the newer set of shrinking taillights, the latest and shiniest upgrades. Chasing, chasing. His wife is at home, lonely. She has chased too. She has chased and chased him until she can no longer bear the thought of chasing.

I imagine that this morning she is in a nightgown that soon will be packed and loaded into the back of her station wagon along with her favorite watercolor, her KitchenAid mixer, and the paisley tie she gave him for their anniversary last year. His bosses will be asking for projections again—always asking for projections— while her taillights shrink down Interstate 49. She will chase the wind to who knows where. It will be bonus time soon, and he'll have only the alimony and a porterhouse steak to show for it.

None of this may be true, of course. It may be only the product of my overactive imagination. In a sense, though, it is all too true. We've all run from some sort of pain; we've all turned our backs and shrinking taillights on something.

I'm lucky. I have a good wife and a happy marriage, save and except for this drinking bit. I am convinced, though, that I am my neighbors and my neighbors are me. We have different problems, different pains. I have the failing health of a shrinking son, and they have the failing health of a shrinking marriage. We all chase, all reach for something to cure this kindred pain, this native groaning. I nurse an appetite for liquor; they nurse different addictions— money, sex, power?

We're all alone together, no matter what shiny face we might be wearing. We are all just people trying to work out our first, best, and only possibility.

I think on these things, the everyday brokenness of this American life, and this is nothing to say of the more visceral kinds of suffering—the hunger, poverty, and prejudices that consume the everyday lives of too many. And we all have our ways of running away.

For me, it is the liquor that silences the noise, mutes the collective groaning of this wounded life. But it blurs the danger and beauty of the world too. It obscures the hippos that guard the far side of the river; it dulls the colors of the dripping sky. In the bottle, the blazing sky has no allure; it presents no threat either. It is only air and empty cloud and occasional wisps of dulling color.

The truth is I'm waiting for the healing God to come and set it all right, to come and rid me of the thirst for liquor. I wonder if he's still in the business of redemption, of healing. Perhaps this is what keeps me up at night.

Who else feels the anxiety of supposing an absent God? Who feels the dread creeping up from behind? Do you know the tightness in your chest, the speeding of the heart? Do you sometimes hear the voices asking what would happen if your friends and family discovered that you doubt God's active, healing, redemptive presence? Do you wonder whether they'll think you a fraud—you, the infidel, the runaway, the doubter?

Yes, if you are looking for a book to entertain you, turn back now. If you are looking for a dose of uncensored honesty, a partner for the coming clean, if you are looking for a sobering exploration of God, maybe we're in this together.

To you, O Lord, I call;
   my rock, be not deaf to me,
lest, if you be silent to me,
   I become like those who go down to the pit.
Hear the voice of my pleas for mercy,
   when I cry to you for help,
when I lift up my hands
   toward your most holy sanctuary.
                                    —Psalm 28:1–2 ESV

There are one million little memories that foreshadow the direction of a life. This is one.

As a boy, I lived down a long North Texas dirt road that divided a series of single-family lots from the expansive cattle ranch of a Texas tycoon. I remember the red dirt, the way the dry southwestern air held dust suspended, how the summer dust covered everything just so, how it dulled all brilliant colors. The scissortail flycatchers dropped from telephone wires and mulberry branches to the tips of thigh-high switchgrass. I remember the mesquite groves, the neon thistles that rose from the hardpan, the dried-out cattle chips that sometimes served as a boy's makeshift frisbee. My young world smelled of dust and sweet dung.

There were no less than three cattle ponds in the field, my favorite of which was the deep hole on the far boundary of the property. It was a safe distance from the eyeshot of my mother, and each summer it would dry into a burnt red crater with soft, swampy sides. It was the largest mud puddle in all of Texas.

It was a boy's dream.

My parents were not wealthy but did the best they could with what they had. One bright Lone Star day, my mother walked into the house with a paper sack and a smile. She had pinched pennies and gone to the store for a bit of shopping. There she bought me an outfit: a secondhand pair of white tennis shorts, a white Izod shirt, a pair of white canvas shoes. There is no doubt that Mother intended to save the bleached-white garb for some particular dolling up of me.

She might have asked me whether I liked them. I might have said yes because I knew it would make her happy, but I don't recall. What I do recall, though, is that my mother had reckoned these clothes as special, and I wanted to get my hands on them.

One searing summer afternoon, I sneaked around back our clapboard ranch home and crept into the shrubs lining the side of the house, new clothes in hand. I stripped down to my jaybird skin, stuffed my old cutoffs and Aggies T-shirt into one of the shrubs, and put on the fresh white outfit. I crossed the road and crawled under the barbed-wire fence with the determination of an explorer who knew the exact location of a new world.

As I slid down the side of the old cow pond, my foot sank deep into the red clay. I felt the pull, the suck of the mud. My shoe held fast; my foot came free. This happened first to my right shoe, then to my left. Undeterred, I made my way to the bottom, where little more than a tablespoon of water had survived the heat of midday. But this was where the mud was the thickest; this was where I wanted to be. This crater was a wild, forbidden kingdom, and I was its king. I built clay men and horses, perhaps a totem or two.

Yet the hole collected the warmth of the sun, and soon I could not resist it. I laid my head back in the rust-red mud as the god of the noon star fired all my creations in nature's kiln.

It was bliss, until I woke.

Panic set in when I first noticed how the mud stained everything—my hands, my arms, my feet, my tennis shorts, even the green alligator on my Izod. It matted my hair in clumps. At first I considered stripping naked and afraid, but then I reconsidered, attempted to run from the bottom of the pit up the steep embankment. I lumbered and lurched, my feet sinking deep into the mud. The mud threatened to suck and swallow me into the earth like the shoes I had already lost. Concern for my soiled clothes evaporated in the high heat. I called for my mother, but she could not hear me. I called for my father, but he was at work.

My kingdom had turned on me. I was stuck. Maybe forever.

Desperate now, I wiggled first my toes, freed them enough to rock my foot from side to side. I pulled, heard suction reversing in a thick slurp. Foot by foot I repeated this until I'd struggled to the top. Free at last, but feeling no thrill of victory, I backtracked across the field, back through the thornbushes and switchgrass, back under the barbed wire. I crossed the dirt road, the outer boundary of the front yard, and then I froze.

There she was waiting with a molten expression. She was at once squinting her eyes into tiny slits and also lifting her eyebrows so high that I thought they might dislocate (if such a thing were possible). Her lips were in the sourest of pursings, and as an adult I now reckon this was her way of keeping from cussing. She was shaking. I knew this because she was holding my cutoffs in her left hand, and the frayed, stringy edges shimmied like grass blades in an earthquake. My new whites were now burnt sienna, and her cheeks were filling with fire at the sight of them.

"Where have you been, boy?" she demanded.

"I don't know," I said. This is my first recollection of the self-preservation instinct.

"Were you at the pond again? And are those your new clothes?"

I looked at her as the blood rushed to my cheeks, as my heart pounded in my temples. Then I did what any self-respecting emotive five-year-old does.

I ran.

I didn't make it far on account of the fact that I was barefoot and my mother was long and lean; she was athletic on rare occasions, but always when necessary. I won't bore you with the details, but let me note that these were the days before the anti-spanking movement had taken firm hold and timeouts had not yet become the punishment *en vogue*—at least, not in Texas. My mother, who had along the way traded my tattered cutoffs for a switching stick, hollered something about "all the bleach in Texas" and dragged me inside by the back of my muddy shirt collar.

It wasn't the last time I visited the pond, but it was the last time I climbed down its red-mudded side. And fearful of the stinging Texas mesquite switch, I always left my white knickers behind.

I have a history of foreshadowed truth; I'd wager we all do. We each have miry holes that lure us, that soil our special outfits and leave us shoeless. Today, I'll make no judgments on your condition, nor will I superimpose metaphor on the particularities of your life. Perhaps you have no affinity for mud holes, for soiling all your clean clothes. Maybe you don't feel the magnets in your hands and feet pulling you through the mud embankments into the deep metal of earthy underground. Maybe you have no urge to wallow in the mud, to rejoin the dust, to become one with the sludge. Maybe you are not stuck in your bottle, your extramarital lover, your money lust, or your bulimic malaise.

This I will say for me, though: I've never seen a set of unstained clothes that didn't beg to be dragged through the mud pit—at least once, even if in secret. Even then, at least in theory, I know how it will end. I know I'll end up stuck, like I find myself these very days. Still, the mud calls.

These days, I've found my feet sinking in the dark gravity of the mud, mud that smells sweet and botanical, hazy and juniper wild. But in the sticking, I see it in truth. This mud is poison for the punishment. This is not the water hole of freedom I'd imagined from a distance. I've found myself stuck, screaming myself hoarse and hoping for rescue from a God who seems deaf or someplace else. And if he should come to my rescue, will he bring a mesquite switch?

"We all have something that we hide behind those whiskey smiles, and those sad cowboy eyes," sings the indie-folk band Carolina Story. I reckon this is true. It's one way of saying that there's a reason we go into the mud pit. There is something that pulls us to the bottom. There is a drive behind addiction. But what is it?

Even tonight I am pulled into my thirst for gin. Gin is just the salve, though. It is not the medicine for what ails me.

It is almost ten o'clock this evening, and I am wallowing in the knowledge that I am stuck. My anxiety rises with the hounding thought that I should *not* be stuck. I am, after all, an accomplished believer in Jesus, a by-God lay minister in a Bible church in Fayetteville, Arkansas. I lead worship for the congregants at my church, host home groups, and discuss theology with my friends. Yes, I am the most accomplished Christian fraud, and this is a thought I'd rather like to quell with liquor tonight. Instead, I'll close my eyes; I'll take long breaths; I'll smell hot jasmine tea and take small sips until the cup is empty. I'm finding that these quiet practices fortify my resolve and help ease my anxieties.

On the front porch, I hear the low hum of Fayetteville night drivers. The neighborhood dogs are quiet this evening, there being no moon at which to howl on account of the low clouds that blew in on the surge of fall. The crickets are singing a colder, more urgent song, and somehow their chirps, the hum of the night drivers, and the quietness of the dogs have concocted a sturdy serenity on the front porch.

I hear the muffled dialogue of one of Amber's television dramas, and I'm thankful for a wife who has given me space to process this tender sobriety. My neighbors have settled into their beds or are waiting for Jimmy Fallon to cross the tube. One neighbor down the street, a churchman, is sitting with his dog in his lap, I imagine. Maybe he's reading his Psalms or saying his quiet prayers. He seems like the quiet praying type.

If I cry for help, will the wind hear me? If I turn my thoughts upward, will there be the invisible father? Will he be here? I'm still not sure I'm ready to find out. I'm not quite sure whether I'm ready to be unstuck.

A gentle rain sets in, bounces from leaf to leaf. The sound is like a thousand fingers tapping, a rhythm rippling through the water and the oak and the night, and my eyes are drawn to the sound. My eyes are drawn up.

The unhinged feeling of sobriety has come. I don't suppose I'm able to put firm language to the unraveling of my nerves just yet. Every afternoon, I feel the burning begin its slow swelter, the tingling, the searing of my skin. It is a house fire of a thing, burning me up from the inside out. In the fire, I hear the siren song of gin calling—it calls and calls—promising me a fire hose full of cold water, something to quench the burning.

I have been told that this kind of unraveling of the nerves is natural, that it'll be around for a while. But if this is meant as consolation, it brings no cheer.

Am I an alcoholic? Alcohol abuser? I'm not sure yet, but I'm finding myself dependent; I'm willing to go that far. My crackling nerves confirm it.

Dependent—let's explore the etymology.

Depend: "to be attached as to a condition or a cause," a figurative use, from Middle French *dependre*, literally "to hang from, hang down."

I imagine the vineyards in Tontitown, the little Italian enclave just a few miles northwest of Fayetteville. The vines spread down trellises and across slow-rolling hills. Up and down, like a river of green, they roll. The spring leaves unfold like broad-palmed hands, raised to the morning sun, dancing in the breeze of the evening. From every branch, the young fruit hang—sugar water dripping from the vine and into the green and purple pearls. The fruit—it hangs down. Its sweetness depends on the aged vine.

This is what it means to be dependent.

This ground has been trod before, and I'm not writing to add to the canon of trite spiritual analogies on vineyards; instead, this is meant as an exploration of word meanings. There are other examples of well-placed dependency: as a baby, I suckled at my mother's bosom; as a child, I was ever-attached to my blankie, needed it to push back the dark dreams; as an adolescent, I sat at the foot of the table, fed by the fruits of my father's labor. The Savior, I think, once hung on the promise of the third-day resurrection. The first saints, strapped to their flaming crosses, hung upon the same hope of resurrection.

Dependence, see, is not always so ill-placed. Dependence can be a good and holy thing. I've misplaced my dependence, though, desacralized the etymology.

Today, I'm not ready to call myself alcoholic. Maybe I'm not yet ready to admit an abusive relationship with the bottle. I recognize the thirsty gin-pangs of the afternoon hour, though. I recognize the way the house fire of anxiety seems to have no other extinguisher. This being so, I reckon I'm ready to at least say it this way: I am alcohol dependent.

Titus came into the room last night. It was half past bedtime, and he stumbled toward me, whimpering. I asked him what was wrong, and he said, "My blankie lost."

"Let's go," I said, hoisting him to my chest. We went to his room, found his blankie by the foot of his bed. I tucked him in, handed him his polyester pacifier. He cuddled it close, smiling. Titus is dependent too. We all learn it so young.

I've become dependent upon something other than the God I claim. And now I want my blankie back.

SEPTEMBER 30

Alcohol dependency runs in my blood. Our family tree—as far back as Adam, best I can tell—has nursed an on-again, off-again, back-on-again relationship with alcohol.

My grandmother, for instance, was a raging drunk. Perhaps that's a crass way to put it, but in the final days of her life, that was the moniker she adopted for herself, and it seems a denigration of sorts not to give her words their proper authority.

Yes, Carol Mouk was an energetic drunk. She once used the word violent to describe it. She was prone to fits of drinking in solitude, and then exploding in community. My mother still weaves stories of Grandmother's drunken loose temper, how she'd sometimes smoosh her obstinate children's faces into pancake stacks when they wouldn't eat, how she'd throw shoes across the room at children in flight. In those days, my mother and uncles were children on the run, but not from flying shoes or frisbee pancakes; they were on the run from the bottle.

My grandfather, a paper salesman by trade, traveled a great deal, his time divided among home, the road, and the office. On account of Grandmother's drinking and my grandfather's absence, mother took a keen interest in looking out for the baby in the family, her little brother, Lee. They were brother and sister, yes, but my grandmother's relationship with the bottle turned normal familial relationships on their head. My mother became a surrogate mother to Lee, protecting him from my grandmother's fits.

I reckon the dynamics of energetic alcoholism throw every family dynamic off kilter.

I never knew my grandmother as a drunk, except for by reputation. Grandmother had done a stint in the crazy ward, where she was dried out good and proper. In the ward, she met Jesus and got religion all in the same whack. I never thought to record her telling her story before her passing, but this I recorded to memory: I only ever knew Grandmother as a fireball, an electric cattle prod, a woman who moved people to their quickest and best moments. After she sobered up, she was an encourager, an AA sponsor, a devoted Episcopalian, and she could throw the "prettiest little parties" in all of northern Louisiana.

Sober, Carol Mouk was a miraculous saint. It's the way I knew her.

In light of my grandmother's history with the bottle, it should not surprise me, I suppose, that my immediate family's relationship with alcohol was standoffish. Generations do that—pendulum swing. I recall seeing my parents drink on only one occasion before I was twenty-one—beer with pizza—and though they never said as much, I think the prohibition days were birthed from some sort of solidarity with my grandmother, who'd up and cold-turkied her drinking problem and hadn't fallen off the wagon.

Although my parents were devoted Christians, they did not excuse this familial prohibition with Scripture or try to force an anti-alcohol theology on my sister or me. Instead, we were told what I have conveyed here about my grandmother's disease, and they left it at that. This seemed good enough reason to avoid alcohol altogether, at least for a time.

But the Baptist church we attended in my teenage years had a different approach. There we were taught of the unholy trinity, the triumvirate of sins that spelled by-God separation from the Crystal Sea and Golden Roads. These sins—premarital sexual relations, voting as a Democrat in any electoral cycle, and consuming alcohol—were surefire badges of the lost. There was, of course, some support in the Good Book for one of the three aforementioned spiritual prohibitions, and it wasn't for alcohol.

The well-meaning pastors tried their best to support prohibition by way of Scripture—"do not gaze at wine when it is red" (Prov. 23:31) or "do not get drunk on wine, which leads to debauchery. Instead, be filled with the Spirit" (Eph. 5:18)—but no one seemed able to explain Jesus' turning water into wedding wine (John 2:1–11). Paul's admonition to Timothy to "use a little wine because of your stomach" (1 Tim. 5:23) was considered a nullity with the advent of Pepto-Bismol. There was no nuance to the issue; instead, anti-alcohol rules were supported by way of reductionist logic.

When it came to alcohol, I never bought the whole-cloth prescriptives of my youth. Even in those days, I reckoned the old Baptists to be fearmongers at best, and intellectually dishonest at worst, though I dared not breathe a word of it.

The Bible had its views on sexuality; that I understood. But I didn't suppose the drink and Democratic ideology to be such bad things, especially if practiced in moderation. After all, moderation gives liberty, and where the spirit of the Lord is, there is freedom (2 Cor. 3:17)!

Freedom in all things!

Freedom in politics! Freedom in alcohol! Freedom, freedom, freedom!

I exercised freedom in and from all things relating to alcohol—even freedom from moderation.

I had my first real drink at twenty-two, two nights before I was married. Embarrassed by the prospect of purchasing convenience store beer, I cajoled my father, experienced closet drinker that he was, to walk from the lakeside hotel where the wedding party stayed to the neighboring EZ Mart. Ten minutes later, he met me and my groomsman Connor—a closet alcoholic in his own right, I later discovered—on the pier overlooking the lake.

Under a waxing moon, the three of us dangled our legs off the pier in Guntersville, Alabama, and talked of life, love, and my coming marriage. I was walking away from the days of boyhood, from the days of endless academia, and I was walking into responsibility, into manhood. The man in the moon half smiled down on the rite of passage as I killed the back third of a beer. I felt the warmth in my chest against the chill of early November. It was an innocent first drink, my first move into the world of adulthood. And once I started drinking, I remember quoting these words of Oscar Wilde and feeling free as I did: "Moderation in all things, including moderation." This is the logic of a future addict. Looking back on it, perhaps I should have resorted to another quote by Wilde, who perhaps was speaking with the wisdom of retrospection himself: "Moderation is a fatal thing. Nothing succeeds like excess."

OCTOBER 1

What if you discover that I'm a fraud, a false flower that, for all its layered colors—the yellows on reds on fluorescent pinks—is made of molded plastic? What if you pluck me from the vase to smell me, find that I'm unrooted, an artifical imposter shoved into a vase of glass marbles?

There are things more strident Christians do not confess within the church house walls. Even if your church is a safe place to out your addiction, your own particular mud pit, here's a confession that's less acceptable even there: I sometimes doubt the very existence of God. I sometimes wonder whether he's nothing but the figment of an overactive imagination. And God, if he were God, could cut through the doubt and speak. Couldn't he?

This thought gives rise to the house fire in my nerves. Here's the thing that drives me to drinking.

⌒

Allow me to share a secret.

In 2013 the question begins to creep: do I have a problem? Amber has asked me time and again whether I've considered cutting back on the bottle, but I tell her with a wink and a smile I'm no quitter. Anything worth doing is worth doing well and all of that. In secret, though, I consider giving up alcohol for Lent in an effort to prove something to myself. I keep it a secret so that if I recant, my hypocrisy will pass unnoticed. After three days of abstinence, my nerves begin to fray. A bout of shingles attacks my torso. I suspend my Lenten devotion and I am five again, wearing my Sunday best to the mud hole. I resurrect my drinking habit within seventy-two hours of Ash Wednesday.

It would be embarrassing, except I avoid the truth. My friends ask about my Lenten commitment, and I tell them it's been a Lenten year already, a year in the ashes of Titus's sickness. I tell them I'm taking Lent to celebrate the life of Christ. I'll break bread and drink wine without regret! I tell my friends I plan to be well-acquainted with the mechanism of celebration come Easter morning.

In earnest, the year with Titus has set me to wondering whether the Lenten season is an exercise in frivolous devotion. The Jesus who made his way to the cross, who rose from the dead—he has not seen fit to bring a resurrection miracle in our hour of need. We've struggled for answers to Titus's sickness, and the pain of the absence of resurrection miracles is too much; I dare not feel it. And so I drink it under the table.

No, I will not spend forty days observing the pain of our own mortality. Instead, I'll skip to the celebration. I'll take the feast of Easter without the lamentation of Lent. I'll drink and drink and drink, and substitute platitudes for rhythmic devotion.

―――――

My mother calls me on Easter Sunday. "He has risen!" she says over the phone on Easter morning. "He has risen, indeed!" I say, hungover and head throbbing. I am relieved that all charades, Lenten or otherwise, have a summing up at one point or another.

But the day—or the charade—isn't over yet.

It's Easter morning, and I lead worship for the two or three thousand at our church, all hungry for the spectacle of celebration. It's an ambitious music set with too many turns for a fogged-up musician. We sing a creed and some spruced-up hymns. Then I embark on a modern resurrection song, and as the congregation is worked into a celebratory frenzy, I climb the scale and sing, "The man Jesus Christ laid death in his grave." As I work my way into a precarious key change, my head threatens to explode, dislocate, and crash onto the stage in a grand fainting spectacle. In the end, I cut the note short, but the congregation bellows on, none the wiser.

After the service, a charismatic couple comes to me, puts their hands on my shoulder, says, "You have a special anointing." Anointing—so that's what they're calling it these days.

———

This morning, I sat in a chair in the corner of the living room and tried to coax myself from sleep with a cup of bad joe. The good-coffee tin had run empty, and I was forced to resort to the coarser-grained stuff that was good enough for my grandpa. Putting off the first sip, I sat as the scent of the Best Part of Waking Up wafted from the side table. There, in early morning grogginess, I fell into a dream.

I was a magician under the hot spotlight. The people were there with their best expectations and their darling children, whose mouths were stained with the pink and blue sugar-residue of cotton candy as they waited to be mesmerized. A circus-suited announcer called my name. "The Great and Powerful," he said before a flash of light and a puff of smoke, before I sprang from the trapdoor under the stage. They gasped. The children laughed as their parents reached to cover their eyes.

I was naked, without my trick deck, my dove, or my "watch me pull a rabbit out of this hat" hat. I was standing there with my words. Only words. I prayed that you'd buy them as some sort of magic, that you'd see them as miracles. But you and I both knew the truth: words are often poor illusions. No matter how I might have hoped otherwise, my words were translucent tricks, cellophane shenanigans unable to hide or otherwise distract you from my nakedness. And you and I both knew this wasn't the man you'd paid good money to see.

Over this last year and a half, I have been searching for God while pretending to have it all together. I've been working in illusions—celebrating Easter when I should have been in Lenten repentance, leading resurrection worship while steeped in a hidden death—and wondering whether God would swing low. I have floundered in this season of Titus's sickness, cried out like the Sunday morning preachers of prosperity tell the congregants to do, all the while wondering if there is a God who will answer, who is not occupied elsewhere, who has not indeed walked away. I have cried out standing, sitting, and kneeling. I've given it a go in my house, at the go-to-church meeting, in the supermarket, at the prayer meeting with good friends, and once (though only in thought) in the middle of an airport. I've found precious little comfort in this cry, and though from time to time I hear the voice that some call the still small voice, I haven't seen the mountains unhinge themselves. I haven't seen Titus healed.

I need some mountains to unhinge.

Do I not have the faith of a mustard seed? Do my pleas fly on a void passport?

Let me be clear: I am never as sure or as strong as my best words might lead you to believe. Are you? I am here now, naked, and I'm not trying to convince you that I am anything other than what I am—a self-medicating, alcohol-dependent straggler, listening the best I know how for the faintest whispers of a God I think I remember.

About the coming clean, about such a naked confession, I can say this: it is an awkward moment. It is a nude plunge into cold water while the women and children watch from the shore. It is the exposition of one thousand embarrassments, the big moment before the crowd when one wishes to recite epic poetry, and nothing but thick-tongued gibberish comes stuttering out.

About the coming clean, though, I can also say this: confession seems like some sort of magic. Not the kind that will garner applause through the mysterious workings of a black top hat—something stranger, something other. Confession by confession, I'm finding who I am and who I am not. Maybe, if I'm lucky, I'll find a good God who will weave a better suit of clothes for me. Maybe I won't soil this set.

I'm not sure if these are the shakes, but my fingers tingle and burn. I can't seem to quench the thirst for a drink, and I'm considering sneaking a nip. I know I need sobriety, but I'm not sure how to go about it.

I know a therapist, dialed his number. I might have a drinking problem, I said, and asked whether he could help me untangle myself. He asked me a few pointed questions. Had I quit drinking? Was I drinking to passing out? Did I have the shakes? Had I been drinking and hiding the evidence? Was it starting to interfere with my law practice? And then he said, "Okay, you're bad enough off. Come on in tomorrow at eleven."

I'm bad enough off. Tell me something I don't know, doc.

Today, over my lunch hour, I met with him for the first time. I told him that I have a drinking problem, though if I had come even a few weeks earlier, I might have admitted only that I have a knack for holding a great deal of liquor. He asked me what I was covering with the alcohol, what I'd been masking. I told him that my son was still struggling, that he needed to be healed and God wasn't answering. I am afraid, I said, of being found out, anxious that the good folks in the good church will think me a fraud because I don't always believe in an active, present, healing God. I don't have enough faith to muster a healing. Sickness, I fear, is the permanent plague of my son's life, of my life.

"That's the fear that leads to questioning God's existence," I said, "and on top of it, my nerves are unraveling and I feel unhinged and half crazy." Gin deadens the nerves, seems to rehinge everything, I told him.

He looked at me with firm, kind eyes and said, "No wonder you have a drinking problem. I don't blame you."

OCTOBER 2

Today, I sat on the therapist's couch, explained the way my nerves are fraying. I told him I cannot stop thinking about alcohol.

"Some anxiety has attached itself to your soul," he said, "and you're using the alcohol to medicate that anxiety. You need to explore it.

"Go into the cave of your soul," he said, or rather that's what I heard him to say. The cave—this is the interior soul-place where my anxieties gather, where they take shadowy form, where I can hear them feeding on bones. It is the place of electric fear.

"You need to normalize the anxieties in the cave," he said. "Visit the dark places of anxiety so often that your brain normalizes the fear and pain; this will allow you to gain mastery over your fear. Then, once the fear is mastered, the light of the truth can come into those dark places."

This sounds like a bunch of pseudopsychological mumbo jumbo with a side of spirituality, if you ask me. I'm in need of a remedy, though, so I went with it. "Practice exploring your anxieties tonight," he said. "Practice facing them."

And so here I am. I've never done this sort of thing, so I'm not sure how to start. The boys are fast asleep, and Amber is out with friends for the evening. Before she left, she held me close, kissed my cheek, asked, "Will you be alright while I'm out?"

I nodded. "Yeah," I said. "My therapist gave me some homework today."

"Alright," she says, "do your homework." She smiles small. "Call me if you need to."

Alone now, I consider my dependency. Were there any gin in the house, I'd be tempted to pour a stiff one, to distract myself with the memories of the honey sky over the Shire River; ah, the memories of my favorite drink. Instead, I am going into the cave; I'm going to explore the anxieties that undergird my doubt in an ever-present God.

I close my eyes in the quiet of my living room and listen. Whispers unhinge me. One whisper in particular.

Oh death, where is your sting?

I know this voice. It is the self-mocking voice that whispered over my son's failing body. It is the voice I heard before I called my sister, before she sneaked a Nalgene bottle of gin into the hospital. This is the voice of the most biting of anxieties.

Oh death, where is your sting?

This is the voice of self-mocking. I've said this with a youthful confidence at the loss of loved ones, wielded it like the best Christian propaganda against suffering. It's a statement that smacks of easy cliché, that rolls off the lips with great confidence—until, that is, you're faced with the sickness of the flesh-of-your-flesh.

The threat of sickness and death has hung over my family. It has been a sword suspended by a horsehair over the head of my youngest son, Titus.

"Oh death, where is your sting?" It's an ironic verse, isn't it? Meant for hope, but we all know the sting of death, yes? The sting of death is in the waiting for God to answer and, in that waiting, hearing nothing at all. It stings us in our own standstill. It's in the doubt, the ways we murder God when we most need him. It's in the fashioning of him into an image powerless either to save or not. It's in the pendency, the space between the mustard seed and the upper crust of the fertile soil. I do not fear my own dying. The sting of my son's potential passing, the thought that God may allow the death of something this good, though? It is not sting; it is scorched earth.

And so I have taken to drowning the best hope I have in the cold, tidal numbness of this boozy sea.

Oh death, where is your sting?

I am in the cave tonight, following this whisper that's so often taunted me, and I shine what little light I can muster in the darkest corner to see what lives behind it. I see a gaunt me, a malnourished, hollowed ghost. I am misshapen, heroin thin, and milk white, and naked. The ghost leans in, smiles yellow, and whispers just as it has before, "Oh death, where is your sting? It's where there is no God. There is only you; you know this."

I am burning again, the fire is pumping from my chest and shooting into my fingertips. It is fraying my nerve endings again. There is no alcohol in the house tonight. I am thankful for this, because were it here, I would abuse it.

Lord Jesus Christ, Son of God, if you're there, come find me. Find me hollow boned, milk white, and heroin thin. Naked as I am, come make me clean.

OCTOBER 3

Come to me, all you who are weary and
burdened, and I will give you rest. Take my yoke
upon you and learn from me, for I am gentle and
humble in heart, and you will find rest for your
souls. For my yoke is easy and my burden is light.
—MATTHEW 11:28–30

The prospect that I am a mocking, God-murdering fraud hangs heavy over me some days. Is the heroin-thin me I found in the cave real? Is it me? Is it my doppelganger? If so, how did we get here? How did the child who once knew—*knew*—the ever-abiding presence of God become so malnourished?

I do not recall a time before I knew the word theology. When I was a child, the adults tossed theologies around like frisbees in the back yard of our Texas ranch house. "What do you think about the theology of grace?" they'd say. Or, "How does that theology account for the spiritual gifts?" It was their best adult effort to sum up an infinite God, to harness the mystic wind. Sometimes, I'd take a break from riding my Big Wheel tricycle down the long drive and I'd listen to their banter. I did not understand them— not really—but I remember wanting to tell them that I could hear God whispering.

I can hear him in my memory still.

The mesquite grove was nestled just beyond that dried up cattle pond where I'd ruined my Sunday best, and on those Texas afternoons that had all the ambiance of a convection oven, the cluster of trees provided an arbor in the midday heat. I'd take my Star Wars action figures to their spacious shade, pretend that Han Solo had found himself stranded on some remote outpost in an unknown system of the galaxy. I'd play until I grew tired of making blaster sounds, and then I'd sit in the quiet.

I'd listen to the wind swishing through the grass in the field, to the rustle in the undergrass where a field mouse was scurrying for cover, spotted by a copperhead or hawk. I'd watch the cows in their slow motion stampede, the great herd of cud-chewers dumb to the world around them. In those moments when the wind cut across the stalks of dying field grass and thistle, when it whistled through the mesquite grove, I remember the acute presence of God.

I am with you. It was less of a hearing and more of a knowing.

I always wanted to share these experiences with the adults, wanted to tell them that I had my own theology. I never did, though. I supposed it might sound silly to the adults who used the big words.

Over the years, I've heard others wield their own big words; I've heard them explain away the notion of a God who whispers to children in the trees. I've heard them call these things syncretistic amalgams of Christianity and pantheism. "God is more systematized, more summed up and proper, and he speaks ever and only through his written word," they say. I'm not sure what to say about that, layman that I am. I suppose I could say, "Go read Paul's letter to the Romans" (Rom. 1:20). Instead, I'll just tell you that I know what I heard when I was five, and we can leave it at that.

My mother was young in her faith when I was a child. She'd gone cold turkey off cold beer and marijuana at some point, and traded in her Aretha Franklin and Janice Joplin for Amy Grant and Sandi Patty. She carried a red guitar around with her to house-church meetings and vacation Bible school, and kept my ear inclined toward songs about the church and Jesus.

There's a church on top of the hill; there's a church on top of the hill;
There's a church, there's a church, there's a church on top of the hill.
There's a pew in the church on top of the hill;
There's a pew in the church on top of the hill.
There's a church, there's a church, there's a church
On top of the hill.

And so on and so forth, *ad nauseum.*

Mother never second-guessed my claim of hearing God in the mesquite trees, never scoffed at the idea that I sensed the presence of God from time to time in the night. I'm thankful for that. She fostered the notion that God was, and would be, a very real presence in my life.

I don't reckon myself special. We were all born into this life hearing the Spirit, weren't we? But most of us, if we're honest, consider offing those mystic notions of God when it suits us. We second-guess the first whispers of God as we grow out of childhood, as we take notice of those ten-dollar theological words that others toss about. Some of us become enamored by the high-mindedness of it all, forget that talking about God is never quite as rich as talking with him. Some of us rationalize this whole God business as a psychological trick, embrace doubt, even if in secret. Some of us do both.

I consider this. Perhaps the child self is the better self, the more attuned self. Wasn't it Jesus who noted that children have special insight (Luke 18:17)? Perhaps it'd do me good to climb a few trees and listen more for the wind these days.

⌐⌐⌐

Since Titus has fallen ill, it has been tough to turn to Scripture. The promises of resurrection, of life abundant—these have all seemed hollow. So when I've read Scripture at all, I've gone straight to the psalms of lament. There I've found comfort in the notion that David—man after God's own heart—was often tortured and confused.

I know, though, that the tides are changing. If I read only the poetic lamentations of David, I'll drive myself straight back to the bottle. So in the last few days, I've begun my morning by reading the Gospels. They bring me back to the simple days of faith, the easy season of Jesus stories I was taught as a child. I'm finding these stories to be a good place to anchor.

Unable to sleep, I woke this morning at 4:30 and made my way to my living-room chair. The house was silent before its usual rumbling into wakefulness, boys tumbling, breakfast sizzling. I read passages in small chunks, stopped and listened until my mind wandered, till I started thinking about the new case at work or holiday plans or about the time Jude got a pencil eraser stuck up his nose. This morning, I heard the distracting voice of the gin calling, calling. In this prone-to-wander place, I stopped. I recentered, and then I prayed.

"I am sorry, Lord. Help my unbelief." I looked back down to the Bible in my lap, and I took another small helping of words to heart. Today, I read the bit about coming to Jesus, the easy-yoked Messiah.

"Come to me," he said, "and I will give you rest" (Matt. 11:28).

I've read these words countless times over the course of my life, but this morning, they came to life in a new way. These words were meant as a promise, I sense, the hope of a present and abiding glory. This assurance comes fast and without warning. Perhaps this is the still small voice speaking?

I consider this promised rest. Is it the rest in the knowledge that God will abide again like he did when I was a child? I have a sense, a knowing that yes, this is it. God will meet me somewhere in this process of drying out.

The evening is winding down, and Amber comes into the room, tea mug in hand. "Are you ready for bed?" she asks. "Yes," I say.

I'll go into the cave again, soon. Tonight, though, I'll lie in bed with Amber. We'll hold each other, and I'll take intentional breaths—deep inhalations, slow exhalations. I'll stare at the ceiling and remember the simple mesquite faith. Then, I'll pray the prayer of the penitent once taught to me by a monastic brother: *Lord Jesus Christ, Son of God, have mercy on me, a sinner. Visit me, the weary underdog.*

So he called to him, "Father Abraham, have pity
on me and send Lazarus to dip the tip of his finger
in water and cool my tongue, because I am in
agony in this fire."

—LUKE 16:24

It has been two weeks since I stopped drinking, and today, I felt the clearing of a fog I did not know was hanging over me. I was playing guitar in the living room, while steeping tea from Savoy, our local specialty tea shop. The aroma of the tea came alive— white tea, hint of strawberry, orange peel—and my fingers began making new connections on the fret board. The music, the aroma, the flavor of it all—it seemed so clear. Everything was a little less lumbering, a little more nuanced.

I've replaced my gin habit with a tea habit. Each night, I fill the electric kettle in the corner of the kitchen, click the button, and watch the blue eye glow until the water begins to bubble. The eye dims, then clicks off when the water reaches its boiling point. I pour the water from the kettle over the wire-mesh tea steeper.

When anxiety begins to radiate from my belly and into my fingers, I brew the tea and pray. I pour water over white teas, green teas, smoked teas, fermented teas. I baptize the leaves, smell the soothing aroma rising with the steam. Sometimes I drizzle honey into the cup from a spoon; I hold the spoon inches above the cup and watch the nectar stretch into thin ribbons. I shimmy the spoon, watch the ribbons dissolve into the water.

Where gin makes all things blur, time smear, I am becoming present in a new way. It is not unlike an awakening.

I've been using this new ritual as a call to prayer. *Lord Jesus Christ, Son of God, have mercy on me, a sinner.* I pray this as the water gives new life to rehydrating leaves.

It's near sacramental, the brewing of oolong or lapsang in the dusky evenings, chamomile before bed. It doesn't quench the fire, but it gives occupation to idle hands that would just as soon mix liquor and tonic as tea and honey. Idle hands are the devil's workshop, and all of that.

It's hard work quelling the cravings for the bottle. It's hard work in process, from mixing cocktails to steeping tea, from drowning anxieties to taking note of them. Occupation takes the place of dissipation.

Even still, I hope for a sobriety that won't feel like so much work. I hope for one that feels more like rest.

Lord, give me rest.

This most recent thirst for a stiff drink has been exacerbated by the fact that my in-laws have come to visit. They've been in town since last night, and this has brought my exploration of the anxieties that haunt my soul cave—the mocking voices of my interior life—to a pernicious halt. My therapist says that going into the cave of the soul should be an everyday exercise. The cave is meant to be a refuge, the place where I might meet God. Unless I clean it of the ghosts, doubts, and anxieties that mock, my therapist might say, I'll continue to struggle with my thirst. I calculate that he will be disappointed in my avoidance of the cave over these last few days.

In any event, my nerves have been lit up more over the last two nights. This is not so much because of the stress of my in-laws' visit (they are good-right Appalachian folks) but because my routine is askew. There is no quiet space for prayers or meditation, for continuing the interior soul work. There is no room for secret snuggles with Amber. Instead, the whole lot of us—Amber's mother, father, sister, and sister's two children (God anoint their rowdy heads)—are crammed into one space, all of us piled on top of each other.

If I am going to face my anxieties and make peace with God, I need my tea steeping and prayer routine. I need the feeling of sacred space. With the chaos, though, I recognize the growing desire for a drink, a salve to numb the noise.

Amber loves these moments with her family, as she should. Her folks have traveled from Alabama to the Ozarks to see her. But my swimming head, my sense of being off-kilter or out of rhythm, is a cautionary cue pointing me to one truth: recovery will be tied to routine; risk of relapse tied to noise. God is hard enough to find in the quietness. In the noise, it seems an impossibility. And the specter of this impossibility brings epiphany: the bottle is a negative pole and I am positive; I cannot control the attraction.

I've not yet said it, but I'm afraid I can name my wrestling with the bottle. Some might call it abuse. I think I might say it different.

"Hello, my name is Seth Haines," and all of that.

Lord Jesus Christ, Son of God, have mercy on me, a sinner. And all of that.

OCTOBER 6

It's always the evenings, when the lights dim and the house quiets, that I feel it most. To describe it as a throbbing is insufficient. It is pent-up energy, primal and magnetic, drawing outward. Always outward. Its pull is like the tide, toward the ocean, toward the moon.

I've felt this kind of energy since I was a boy. This is the family energy. I'd like to describe it as something less dramatic, and perhaps others in my family would. They might call it a nervous tic, an itch. We are prone to the constant leg bounce, the shin shimmy, which, incidentally, drives my wife crazy at dinner gatherings and movie theaters. There is and always has been a present discomfort, a stirring tension. I suppose it's in the blood.

This is what my DNA gave me.

My grandfather wrestled with this same energy; he was a man never at rest. He was equal parts family patriarch, successful businessman, charismatic leader, scratch golfer, house chef, and the consummate North Louisiana conservationist. George Mouk was a man pulled to passion. He was a unifier, a developer, a solution-oriented and outcome-determinative man prone to tell you what you ought to do. And every night, he dulled his obsessive drive, his own pent-up energy, and the worries that came with them, with stiff gin drinks.

I remember the botanical scent on his breath, he pulling me into his lap when I was a boy, rocking in an old wicker chair overlooking the bayou. "Sit here, boy," he'd say, "and let me tell you about my namesake." St. George was a war hero during the

Crusades, he said. A fierce warrior, a leader of men, he was pulled toward great things too.

St. George once found a damsel in a field, my grandfather told me, she clothed in a wedding dress, bound hand and foot. The maid was to be sacrificed to the dragon, the beast that tormented the girl's village. No sooner had the maiden declared her plight than the dragon appeared, blue blazes flaring from his upturned snout.

Grandpa Ducky—we called him this on account of the bayou ducks he fed every evening—leaned in, fire on his breath. "St. George was undaunted," he said. "He charged and lanced the dragon in the heart. He straddled the head of the dragon, roaring and bucking as he was, and with a clean stroke, he separated the beast's massive skull from his neck." He paused, let the story settle as the mallards splashed down into bayou water from the western sky. Then, in the cicada crescendo on the banks, he said, "You can slay dragons, boy. You can set things right."

My grandfather's storytelling was always marked by the scent of Gordon's gin, a dry London swill that, when mixed with tonic, tasted like an evergreen forest fire and quinine. Patriarch as he was, noble as he was, when we visited his house, it was the only drink.

Amber traveled with me to meet Grandma and Grandpa Ducky over Christmas break of 1998.

Standing in the kitchen one evening, he grinned across the room and with paternal demand boomed, "Amber, make me a gin and tonic." This was Amber's first test, her first running of the family gauntlet.

My mother balked, said, "She won't know how you like it, Daddy."

"I bet you my hat, my glasses, and my overcoat she will," he drawled.

Amber poured a double (perhaps a triple) into a red Solo cup and splashed a bit of tonic on top. No need for the lime, he had told her, so she had dispensed with the pleasantries. He held the cup high, toasted, "Laissez les bons temps rouler," then sipped, eyes rolling into the back of his head, and he hummed, then broke into a baritone rendition of "A Pretty Girl Is Like a Melody." Amber blushed. Grandpa had a way with the ladies.

He carried a green ammo crate in the back of a white Ford Expedition. It was his survival kit, his overnight stash: a bottle of Gordon's, pickled onions, a few limes, Schweppes tonic water, and a bottle of Dry Sack sherry. ("You never know when sherry season might sneak up on you," he'd say with a wink, especially in the days after my grandmother's passing.) This was his crate of courage, his magic box. It was endearing, part of his persona and our family lore.

There was never a more joyous group than anyone under the influence of his libations. He was a jubilant imbiber, a loose fellow who'd tell secret stories of the war and breaking codes and young lovers. He'd flirt with the granddaughters-in-law, would tell off-colored jokes in that aw-shucks manner afforded eccentric and accomplished southern elders. It was Gordon's gin and tonic that most often contributed to these memories, some of my fondest of him.

My grandfather bequeathed me his prominent nose, his flat backside, and his penchant for Gordon's and Schweppes. I took what afforded him a measure of evening joy and made it the terrible-useful. It quelled the fear, the anxieties that come with fatherhood, steady employment, and more unfixable things.

I used it to quell the fear of losing a son.

In the summer of 2012, as I watched Titus fail to thrive, I thought of my grandfather, who had already made his way to the Call up Yonder. It was impossible not to think of him, to think of St. George the dragon slayer, with every glass of gin I drank. Yet it wasn't just a children's tale anymore. Dragons, I knew, were very real things.

Titus was floundering, his disease an ever-present shadow, and I had no faith to summon a mortal wound. Instead, the drink took the edge from my waning faith, from the pain of the dragon's teeth sinking deep.

Some foes seem invincible, no matter what our grandfathers' folk stories tell us. I suppose we all have these foes. You know, those things that haunt and haunt and haunt?

Tonight I'm sipping tea again, allowing the smoky finish of lapsang to linger, but my brain is misfiring, telling me that the juniper fire of gin is a better fit for this stage of life. Juniper fire is a jealous mistress, and it's all I can do not to miss her.

I have quit Gordon's and tonic, and strange as it may sound, I feel like I've betrayed a family trust. Perhaps my grandfather would be proud. Perhaps he'd feel judged. I don't know.

Prone to wander, Lord, I feel it.

Lord Jesus Christ, Son of God, have mercy on me, a sinner. Here's my heart, Lord; take and seal it.

5:58 a.m.

Before the day's thoughts have had the opportunity to pile into a great snowball, a gathering mass of worry that sweeps me up and spins me over and over and over, I am thinking about a text sent by my friend Joel.

"In Mark 5," he types, "Jesus sent the demons from the demoniac. No man could restrain him. Only Jesus."

> They came to the other side of the sea, into the country of the Gerasenes. When He got out of the boat, immediately a man from the tombs with an unclean spirit met Him, and he had his dwelling among the tombs. And no one was able to bind him anymore, even with a chain. . . . And He was asking him, "What is your name?" And he said to Him, "My name is Legion; for we are many." And he began to implore Him earnestly not to send them out of the country. Now there was a large herd of swine feeding nearby on the mountain. The demons implored Him, saying, "Send us into the swine so that we may enter them." Jesus gave them permission. And coming out, the unclean spirits entered the swine; and the herd rushed down the steep bank into the sea, about two thousand of them; and they were drowned in the sea.
>
> —Mark 5:1–13 NASB

"Only Jesus," Joel says.

This is a good thought, and I consider it, though I also know I have been running from Jesus for a long time now. I have fashioned a noose around the neck of an efficacious Jesus; I swung him from the rafters at a children's hospital in Little Rock when I stopped praying in earnest for Titus's healing. The Jesus of Mark 5 has never had the opportunity to meet me, the demoniac on the far shore of the Gerasenes. This present-day, healing Jesus—he is dead to me. Or maybe it's my faith in him that is dead. It is hard to tell.

This doubt in Jesus the healer—I suppose it's been this way for most of my life.

Even to type this is painful, and it would be even more painful if I did not believe that I am not alone, that there are so many who, if they were honest, would admit the same thing. So many of us have tied up Jesus, have pretended to kill him proper. Granted, there is no comfort in mass delusion, but I figure someone ought to come out of the closet, and it may as well be me.

Here I am, murderer and doubter.

6:04 a.m.

Titus has walked into the room this morning. He has come in, red blankie in tow, and he lies in front of the couch. He is rail thin, even one year after the hospital, after feeding tubes and dietary changes, after appointments with the best medical professionals in the state. In the last week, we have found ourselves again mired in another season of quandaries. Not only has Titus stopped gaining weight, he has begun losing it again. This is maddening.

A few weeks ago, Titus began hacking something awful, and after a round of X-rays, the local pediatrician thought it might be best to send Titus back to Children's Hospital for an arthroscopic peek into his lungs and a meeting with the pulmonologist. Days later, Titus sat in the hospital waiting room, asking Amber for chicken nuggets, when the specialist entered.

"You want some chicken nuggets, little guy?" he asked.

"Chicken nugs," Titus said, eyes brightening.

"Right this way," said the doctor, and he led him behind the swinging doors where a team of anesthesiologists waited in ambush for our stick-legged son. The team scooped him up, slapped a laughing-gas mask on him, and put him under. The good doctor (occasional white liar though he may be) sent a mechanical worm into Titus's lung. The worm, equipped with camera and pincers, found a popcorn kernel that Titus had aspirated some weeks before. The doctors removed the kernel as if playing the childhood game Operation, but the procedure created a small nick in the lung tissue, one the pulmonologist said may cause irritation for a few days.

Titus coughs this morning—hacks, really. Even still, he smiles as he rubs the corners of his blankie. He is a happy boy. I see him, bobble head atop a toothpick body. His head is in the eightieth to ninetieth percentile, while his body length remains in the fifth to tenth percentile, and his weight in the negative percentiles. This is the math that mocks faith, the equation that doesn't add up to a healing God.

I can feel the fires of anxiety creeping. There is fear here. Why can't Titus seem to get on the right track? Why isn't he being healed? Why can't he eat popcorn without sucking a kernel down the wrong pipe? Why can't he hack the intruder out? Why are so many anomalies baked into Titus's DNA?

I think back to Mark 5, to the demon possessed of the Gerasenes, and in this moment I wish I could be delivered from the demons of doubt. But in truth, I identify less with the demoniac and more with the swine. Unsuspecting as they are, ignorant as they are, the little piggies make perfect demon temples.

My therapist tells me that the nervous fire that makes me feel insane is nothing more than my body's limbic response. Each time I think of Titus's sickness, when I remember the days at Arkansas Children's, my amygdala responds and tells my body to release adrenalin. Fight or flee, it says. The adrenalin rides in on a rough wave of cortisol, the stress hormone, and the hormones wash over me, prepare me for the next battle.

The amygdala is the storehouse of emotional memory, my therapist says; he supposes it is the home of what we have come to call the soul. It is the most protected part of the brain, sitting between the temporal bones located behind the ears. It helps in the processing of life's stressors, sends the signal to "stand and fight like a man!" or "run for your life!" This, he says, came in quite handy when the cavemen stumbled across the pad-footed track of the saber-toothed tiger. Or St. George's dragon, I think. "But you," he says, "have learned to see saber-toothed tigers everywhere, and instead of facing the pain and realizing that your son's sickness is no such animal, instead of seeking solutions, you numb the response with alcohol."

And here is my precarious position: instead of facing pain with faith in the Christ who promises rest, I have learned to avoid it all by way of substitution. I've traded the abiding rest of Christ (if such a thing is real) for the temporary rest of liquor.

I have become Jonah, a man in rebellion swallowed into the hollow belly of something other.

Yet I will name it now. I think I can.

Lord Jesus Christ, have mercy on me, a running rebel.

Lord Jesus Christ, have mercy on me, an addict.

6:22 a.m.

I've turned on *Sesame Street* for Titus. He loves Elmo, and the red puppet-face is going on about birthdays and cackling in high-pitched joy. A kazoo carries an annoying but happy melody. Titus laughs, then coughs.

The therapist has told me to turn in to the pain, to see that it is a normal part of the human experience. "Face the grief you have over Titus's sickness and allow yourself to heal." It seems ridiculous that fear and grief could be so crippling, seeing that my son is alive, drinking juice and laughing at Elmo. But the human heart is an awkward mess, and the brain even more so, at least as far as mine are concerned.

Lord Jesus Christ, Son of God, have mercy on me, a sinner. And give me rest.

OCTOBER 9

Every morning, I slink out of bed before five o'clock and trudge through the thick hallway carpet. This morning, I walked past the boys' rooms, all four of them bundles of potential energy.

Quiet in this house is a miracle, so I make the most of it. I settle into my reading chair, then venture into the cave of the soul. This is the inner sanctuary, the place meant for sober quiet. I've allowed others here, though, and this morning, I hear a faint murmur, a rustling, a whisper. There are ghosts in the cave, versions of me I'd rather drown than face, and they prod me with their accusations. But into the pain my therapist says I must go, and so I do.

In the stillness, I gather my thoughts, ask God to show me the genesis of my pain. Where did I lose faith in an abiding God? What is the source of my despair over Titus's sickness?

———

I remember the sounds of summer cicadas, their songs rising like a crescendo in the evening. These are the sounds of my childhood, the first songs I remember hearing when we moved from Texas to Arkansas. In the Ozark summer, the cicadas chirp at near deafening decibels; they are the chorus that sings the sun to sleep.

The summer before my seventh birthday, we left behind the Texas mesquite groves, the cattleman's field, and the oversized mud puddle, and our family made our way north and into the foothills of the Ozark mountains. My father had been transferred to work in the home office of a transportation company, and so it was Arkansas or bust.

These mountains, however, were not kind to my asthma. My attacks worsened in the less arid climate, and I remember the fits were like choking, like breathing through a pinched straw. We found a country doctor, a good man who would open the office at midnight to administer a breathing treatment or an adrenalin shot, but the constant attacks drove my parents to desperation. And as any parent knows, desperation will drive you to search for miracles.

In Texas, we'd attended a charismatic Baptist church that believed in signs and wonders. My parents had come to faith from their own stolid traditions—my mother having been raised Episcopalian and my father in the Church of Christ—and they rejected the notion that God could not perform miracles. And so, on a Tuesday night in the sweltering Arkansas heat, my mother and father decided it might be a good idea to take me to see a charismatic faith healer who was appearing at a local Assembly of God church.

The road to the church meeting was a country road, and we drove past grazing pastures and junkyards, windows down so as to hear the cicada songs. I do not recall whether my parents spoke or whether the radio played, but I remember the heat and the dust and the sense that we were driving toward something weighty.

We pulled into the gravel parking lot of the massive sanctuary, its steep roof like a circus big-top tent. Cars filled the lot, and the people were all abuzz, entering the sanctuary like bees into an anointed hive. We were there, the whole lot of us, to see a globe-trotting faith healer whose weapons of warfare were a ten-pound Bible, a gallon jug of olive oil, and an ensemble of hallelujah singers dressed in blue choir robes trimmed in gold.

A stringy first grader, I watched as the faith healer whipped the crowd into a frenzy of the not-for-Sunday sort. He might have preached about healing by the stripes of Jesus, or he may have spun his healing theology from the story of the hemorrhaging woman who touched Jesus' garment hem. I don't recall. But the Tuesday night crowd was lapping it up, ready to jump into any Pool of Bethesda they could find.

As the congregants filled the blessing lines, I asked my mother whether it was time. "Not yet, honey," she said. "Let's wait until the service is over." I obliged her because I didn't feel sick in the moment. I was breathing mighty fine. After all, didn't Mom and Dad always make it right? Didn't they always bring healing of a different sort, what with the inhalers and pills and the occasional breathing treatment? The way I saw it, they had this healing bit covered, but if this faith healer could deliver a more permanent solution, I was game.

We endured the prayers over the crippled, lame, blind, and deaf until the last congregant slipped down the aisle and toward the exit, his oil-smeared forehead gleaming under the house lights. We went forward, and there we stood before the lanky evangelist, tall in his gray suit. He asked what type of healing I'd come for. I said that I wanted rid of my asthma. He smiled, showing too many porcelain-white teeth, laughed, and said that nothing is too big for Jesus.

"With enough faith, all things are possible."

He marked my forehead with an olive oil cross and prayed that my lungs would open, claimed my healing by the precious blood. "We rejoice in this boy's healing even now. Amen," he said.

The evangelist stooped and looked into my eyes. Did I feel the presence of the Holy Spirit, he asked? I told him, "I think so," but that was a lie, the kind a kid tells grown-ups who are doing the best they know how. The truth was I didn't feel anything. There was no tingling, no warmth of healing, no rush of Holy Spirit ecstasy. I knew nothing had changed, and in that moment, with the weight of adult hopes and expectations hanging on the sufficiency of childlike faith, an exchange took place. I bartered my mustard seed of childhood faith for the bitter seed of doubt.

This seed grew in shadow for years. Even after the healing service, there were asthma attacks so severe that I was taken to the emergency room. There were adrenalin shots and breathing treatments. There were years of steroids. I was never healed.

The continuing sickness suffocated my faith. The sickness grew to mock me. *Oh death, where is your sting?*

Yesterday I rode my bike in the breaking weather of the turning fall. The air was cool, and as I rode by the mucky pond with the solitary cypress tree, allergens pricked my lungs like a hundred needles. My bronchial passages began closing; the shrieking wheeze set in. A common bike ride served as a reminder: I have never been healed. Since the earliest days of my childhood, my faith has never been good enough—not really.

So I reach for things other than faith: the medicine; science and surety.

On my bike ride, I reached for the inhaler in the back pocket of my cycling shirt, pressed the canister and breathed deep. Science is my healer. It opens my air passages and allows my legs to pump harder, faster. Science can be a savior. *Yes, that's it.*

My hope has been built on nothing less than these kinds of modern marvels. I do not believe in a healing, present God. It is no wonder, then, that I have little faith for Titus outside of modern medicine.

⌒

Oh death, where is your sting?

In my memory, the sting is crouching behind my lingering doubts, behind the undoing of a childlike faith. I can hear the faith-healer preacher all these years later in the interior soul-spaces. Our histories never really evaporate, do they? He is here in the cave that is supposed to be my refuge, charcoal suit camouflaging him against the blackness. He is a floating head, a disembodied smile. He spits prooftexts at me like arrows in the dark.

"Faith like a child, like a mustard seed," he says. He smiles, anoints my head. Not with oil. Seeing with adult eyes, I know better. He anoints me with fire-hot doubt that sears my forehead like a branding iron. I can feel his thumb pushing into the forehead of my memory. He is leaving his mark, and I know it.

I consider him and am again a stick-thin child, standing gape mouthed and wide eyed. There is the preacher, kneeling and looking into my eyes. He sighs and, hand on my shoulder, pronounces, "Faith like a child? Pretend if you will, but you've never had it. You've always been marked by the doubts of a man."

These are voices that haunt from my history. These are the voices on a vicious, repetitious loop.

Oh death, where is your sting?

The sting is here, in the cave of my own soul, and because I've never confronted it, it has been bleeding my faith dry. My disbelief in a present healer did not start with Titus. It has been lurking here for years, hidden behind my various and sundry coping mechanisms, behind my adult rationalizations, dependence upon science, and various theological constructs. Yes, healing is both miraculous and rare. So rare that I've never seen it. And if God is no longer a present healer, is he present at all? Has he ever been?

Is God with us?

If faith starts as a mustard seed, maybe doubt does too.

―――

Perhaps you know the feeling of fraudulent faith, of adult disbelief? Perhaps it is rooted in your childhood too?

The son who was molested; the daughter who lost her daddy when she was just a girl; the wife whose husband is a disengaged, overachieving, road warrior of a salesman; the husband whose wife has been in an affair for all these years. There are some who have been used and discarded by the church, others who do not believe their worth, their beauty, that they are loved—much less liked—by God. There are those who have been beaten, those who are poor, those who are ever and always on the lesser side of advantage.

Anyone who's been one of these, who's felt the sting of unanswered prayer, shares the same searing question.

Where did our God go?

I have found God ineffective in answering healing prayers—or rather unwilling to remove disease from me or my family, anyway. Why hasn't God healed my asthma? Why won't he heal Titus? These questions are a real and present thorn in my flesh, the thorn that gives rise to the sting of doubt. The sting brings the fire of nerves unraveling, leads me to believe that I am a fraud. I proclaim the power of a risen Jesus while harboring private doubts about the very same power. These fired-up nerves beg for relief that no amount of gin could ever quench. I could try other coping mechanisms, I suppose: women, work, the pursuit of money or power, pornography, exercise, eating too little, eating too much, accolades and applause and Instagram likes. There are too many coping mechanisms to list. You know this. Right?

The bottle is not the thing. The addiction is not the thing. The pain is the thing.

The jig is up. My cover-up is threadbare. I can hide no longer. Not even from myself.

So, dear God, let's begin the process of removing the thorns of unbelief. Let's begin the process of dismantling every coping mechanism, of setting them out in the rain to rust.

Lord Jesus Christ, Son of God, have mercy on me, a sinner. I do believe. Help my unbelief.

OCTOBER 10

When as a child you're held at shotgun point by the healing power of God, your view of God's mercy, the effectiveness of prayer, and the reality of faith trembles. And what happens to that faith when the things you believed with such innocence turn out to be a ruse? What happens when childlike faith is not enough? You may begin to compensate for the sickness, may begin to fake wellness in an effort to avoid facing pain, suffering, or disillusionment. (Which is to say nothing of disappointing the hard-believing, well-meaning, faith-wielding adults.) You may dive deeper into the appearance of faith, putting on the airs of holiness. You dive headlong into knowing the ancient stories, memorizing Scripture, or explaining the workings of the world with a religious flourish. These things, in and of themselves, may not be bad, but if they are only the vestiges of false faith?

I know this false faith.

After the faith-healing incident, my parents began attending a small Baptist church that did not believe in charismatic giftings. These Baptists were a temperate bunch and seemed to believe less in the miraculous power of God and more in the practical power of personal holiness. They cautioned against sin, yes, but they also cautioned us against dangerous theologies: speaking in tongues, dreams and visions, physical manifestations of healing. These more mystical expressions of the faith are subject to human whim, we were told, and human whims pave the road to perdition. And so we were instructed in the ways of a "by your own bootstraps" kind of faith.

By your bootstraps, by God. By effort, by God.

In the school of bootstrap theology, children learn straining and striving. They learn a responsible, if not tired, faith. The sin prohibitions promote personal holiness, and personal holiness kept our Sunday best from tarnish, and in turn, it kept us from tarnishing the glory of God. After all, the Christian faith isn't all about us; it is about God, we were told. And told. And told.

The gifts of God, the mystical ones like healing and speaking in tongues, had, for the most part, ceased. Healing was for man's glory (perhaps his vanity), while suffering created the patina of brassy saints. Suffering, after all, produces endurance, and endurance produces hope, and hope produces character, and so on and so forth (Rom. 5:3–4).

At seven, I was learning to strive after holiness to the exclusion of healing; even then, I think, I was learning to be tired.

It might be easy to discount this now as whitewashed religion. But I admit there was good hiding behind this conservative religious practice. Our minds were trained toward reason. We were taught the Scriptures passed down from saint to saint. We were supported by parents who wanted nothing more than to keep us safe from a world full of dangers.

But the hope of healing? I was kept safe from that too. I was protected from the disappointment of my own expectations, from a God who might fail my more childish mystical hopes. And so I was never taught the doctrines of healing, whether spiritual or physical. Sure, we gave lip service to the gift. God *could* heal if he wanted, and so on and so forth. But God, in those days, had chosen to abstain for the most part. Healing and wonders were not part of his normal routine, and many preached that God had ceased dealing in signs and wonders. "When the perfect comes, the imperfect will pass," they said, the perfect referring to the canonized Scripture and the imperfect referring to signs and wonders.

And so we gave God the "if it be your will" way out of miraculous intervention, which seemed a workable solution, a theological counterbalance to stories of healing in the Scriptures and the palpable lack of it in our own bodies. In this, we took some measure of pious pride too. After all, isn't physical suffering just another way to learn dependence on God?

The absence of a healing theology grew into a monster, though, and it sank its teeth into our religious practices. We were not people of healing. Like our God, we were a stingy sort and held spiritual healing just outside the grasp of sinners. What of mercy? What of leading people into the healing rest of God?

⌒

If you are not a people that believes in healing, what framework is there to reconcile a sick world?

In my teenage years, a friend—a simple ray of light, one of the rare beautiful—found herself pregnant. It was, she knew, an imperative that the child be raised under a Christian roof. And so, with no second thoughts, she and the father were engaged and approached the church to choose wedding dates. The church building was available; the preacher was not. I wonder whether the taint of sexual promiscuity was too scarlet a letter.

Unwed pregnancy was a misstep, I inferred, not even God could heal.

These days, some twenty years later, I still see my old friend around town. She did not receive the blessing of our local body in her teenage wandering, nor did she find healing or restoration in dogmatic pragmatism. Did she sense the abiding presence of a near God in her isolated wedding ceremony?

I wonder whether she's found healing for these certain emotional wounds now. I wonder whether she found another way to wholeness.

⌒

Some have the scarlet letter of affliction tattooed on them by their community, and they hope to hide it under long sleeves. Others pin affliction on the vest, wear it like a badge of honor.

In college, I was an intern at a megachurch spectacle outside of Atlanta, Georgia. Among other things, I employed my limited musical talents as a member of the band that led the Wednesday night youth service. One particular Wednesday, in an asthmatic fit, my lungs seized and my fingernails blued. I pushed through the set and then sped to my summer home, where I found relief in my inhaler.

Prayers for healing were not in my wheelhouse—not anymore— and I suppose that in some respects, I didn't need them to be. In the developed world, why reconcile the spiritual confluence of sickness and healing when science and medicine make easy work of maladies? Why resort to the magic of a voodoo healer when a pill or puff can bring release?

I sat with my pen that night, and in an attempt to explain away my need for healing, I theologized. Instead of asking God for healing, my theological constructs dictated that I treat the sickness as a lesson from God—God, the vindictive teacher. Sometimes sin constricts our spiritual windpipes, I told myself, but when we deal with this sin, we're allowed to worship with freedom; we're allowed to worship like breathing. I should be grateful, really, that God gave me this physical reminder that I so needed his grace, and that only by his grace could I worship. And then I turned this existential theologizing into a worship song.

Let me breathe in your Spirit and exhale your praise.

There are things I reckoned ego-centric, things with which a savior should not be bothered. Requests for physical relief, white weddings for jet-black sinners—these were self-centered prayers to a God who promised salvation through suffering, right? At least, I thought so then.

Sometimes I still do.

As I sit in my chair and consider the past, wounds open—the emotional kind. I am sick with misapplied understandings of Jesus. I am sick with doubt. I am sick with nihilism, with fear of confessing my doubts. I am sick with the bottle. I am sick and in need of healing.

This morning, though, for the first time, I see my sickness as an invitation to a new way forward. I'm reading these words from the gospel of Luke: "Jesus answered them, 'It is not the healthy who need a doctor, but the sick. I have not come to call the righteous, but sinners to repentance'" (Luke 5:31–32).

I'm sick enough to need a physician. This morning, I will ask for healing for the first time.

Lord Jesus Christ, Son of God, have mercy on me, a sinner, and heal my sick lungs, my sick heart, and my sick son.

By day, I am a lawyer in a large Arkansas firm. Like animals, lawyers group in packs. Lions have their prides. Crows have their murders. Lawyers have their bars. I've always supposed that at the convocation of the first group of lawyers, one of the members posed the question, "Exactly what shall we call ourselves whence we are gathered in a group of three or more?" Another raised a stiff drink, chuckled, and noted, "Why not a bar?" This is, of course, a hypothetical account, but if the shoe fits and all of that.

Yesterday evening, my office hosted a local chamber of commerce event. The caterers and bartenders began to arrive at four, began to arrange the food and booze tables for Business After Hours. There were two booze tables, each with a pair of green Tanqueray bottles. The limes were cut; the sting of citrus hung like perfume near the table. I heard the crack and hiss of the tonic-water bottles, the prelude to the unwinding of bankers, lawyers, and business leaders.

It has been almost three weeks since my last drink, and the burning fire is not as constant. Now it sneaks up on me at the most inopportune times, which is what happened the moment I saw the twin bottles of gin. My stomach fluttered, heart sped. Perhaps this is the feeling of new singleness in the presence of an old and favored lover? Perhaps this is the blinding thirst of nostalgia? Perhaps it is nothing more than the physiological draw to the surefire numbing?

No one should crave poison, but addiction is about unlearning nature's cues, and the body is far slower a learner than the mind.

Hunter attended the event—client and friend, an observant

fellow with a healthy tolerance for the machinations and gamesmanship of business relationships. Knowing that I've decided to part ways with my most favored mistress, he found me in the corner of the room, looked down at my napkin-shrouded Diet Coke, and asked how I was.

"I'm making it," I said.

"You're doing well," he said, "but you look like you're jonesing for a stiff one." Hunter has a way with words. Then he added, "Why don't you get out of here? You've made your appearance. There's a difference between being a gracious host and torturing yourself."

A business acquaintance moved into our conversation with the gusto of a used car salesman, looked down at Hunter's cup. "Whatcha got there?" he asked, hoping to compare liquor notes with Hunter. Hunter looked at me, drew a line down to my Diet Coke with his eyes, then looked to our new compatriot. "Tea," he responded.

It was a naked lie.

There was whiskey in Hunter's cup, and we both knew it. In that moment, though, he had chosen a more Franciscan way— make me an instrument of peace, he may well have prayed. Hunter understands the power of words, knows that there is power in the confession of some things, and power in the withholding of others. The word whiskey would have been a subtle prod, a titillating reminder of bygone days, and he spared me from it.

There are some in this world with a gift for understanding the internal gyrations of pain. There are some with rudimentary but well-practiced gifts of healing. I suppose I could learn a thing or two from men like Hunter.

Lord Jesus Christ, Son of God, have mercy on me, a sinner. And make me an instrument of your peace.

The apostles said to the Lord, "Increase our faith!"
He replied, "If you have faith as small as a mustard
seed, you can say to this mulberry tree, 'Be uprooted
and planted in the sea,' and it will obey you."
                                        —LUKE 17:5–6

I did not write this weekend. Though one might wonder whether
the gap between the dates of this entry and the last is the result of
a relapse, it is not. I rode the wagon this weekend, difficult though
it was.

My thirst for liquor is burning less by the day. I've found a
secret to overcoming the anxious desire. I've prayed the Jesus
Prayer time and again—*Lord Jesus Christ, Son of God, have*
mercy on me, a sinner. Sometimes I add some additional content: *I*
cannot control my thirst; fill me with better desires. These prayers
have become a constant anchor, and I find that it is working some
kind of good magic in me.

Magic?

This seems an offensive word to the modern Christian. After
all, many a heretic found himself in dire straits attempting to conjure the miracles of Jesus like a mad magician. Many a preacher
has crushed the faith of children in the attempt to make asthma or
cancer into a grand disappearing act, Jesus' name invoked like a
magic word. Don't those ask-and-receive, health-and-wealth sorts
practice a type of Jesus magic? Maybe.

Perhaps magic is not the right word. Perhaps I'm dealing, instead, in mystery.

Yes, I feel the working of prayer, the way it is communion with the original Natural Force, the Force who gave birth to all forces and holds all things together (Col. 1:16–17). I feel the prayer drawing me to peace, producing something of a miracle. If this could be described as anything other than holy mystery, it'd have to be called conversion or healing, and I've not given myself to these words yet.

Healing is such a difficult concept.

Today, I visited my therapist, and he asked whether I've turned in to the pain.

"Yes," I told him, "it's been a regular carnival of unicorns and cotton candy."

He did not laugh. "What have you found?"

I explained the way all things seem to connect when I explore the darker places in my heart, how all tributaries run to a particular and single source. My anemic self, my structured dogmas and disbelief in the healing power of God over my son—it all goes back to the faith healer, to the powerless anointing olive oil he purchased from the Piggly Wiggly.

"Good," he said, "tell me how you feel about that."

I considered it, and my stomach turned. I ran short of breath. I felt untethered, dangled over a great pit by the hand of a god who is either capricious or not there. This, of course, I could not articulate, and instead I said, "When I think about the faith healer, I can't breathe; there's fire, an empty feeling."

"Okay. What else?"

I could not bring myself to admit the feeling of abandonment, but it was there. I considered this sense of God abandonment. What if I never normalize this sense, or what if I do—what if I come to the conclusion there is no God? Worse yet, what if I conclude there is a God, but that he doesn't meet me in my dark places?

I gathered the courage to say what I mean to my therapist, and it's this: there have been two times that I've offered specific requests for God's healing. Once, I was a child with faith bigger than a mountain, and I asked God to move what I considered to be a mustard seed. Once, I was a father with faltering, flailing faith like a mustard seed, and I begged God to move what seemed to be a mountain. On both occasions, I might as well have saved the breath with which my prayers were uttered.

This thought is terrifying.

This evening, I am reflecting on the prayers of a father. Before I gave up the ghost on the business of prayer for Titus, I prayed like a good father would. I prayed like Jairus, the synagogue official in the Gospels who came to Jesus. "Heal my daughter," he said, but along the way, Jesus was sidetracked by a hemorrhaging woman who reached out in unclean faith to touch the hem of Jesus' robe. The woman was healed the instant she grasped the hemline, and Jesus, sensing the healing moment, stopped. "Who touched my robe?" he asked. "I felt the power of God going out from me, healing someone with grand faith."

I imagine Jairus. "Yes, yes," he may have been saying, "but let's get on with it. We have precious little time." Perhaps he wondered whether Jesus' healing power had been spent on the bleeding woman. Maybe he questioned Jesus' ability to conjure two miracles in a day. And as fate or divine providence would have it, in the moment that Jesus stopped to heal the woman, Jairus's daughter passed. A house servant approached, told the men that the little girl had been taken to the underworld. "Don't worry," Jesus said, "she is just asleep. Let's go" (Luke 8).

I think of Jairus, how he took Jesus' words at face value,

without regard for his servant's grim news. Was he a man of great faith? I reckon him to be. It is this kind of man who trusts a doctor even after death has overtaken life.

In the days leading up to Titus's stint at Arkansas Children's Hospital, I prayed a great "come by here" prayer, asked for a healing miracle. My petitions lifted hollow, smelled like nothing in God's throne room. They were unnoticeable, dull, and lackluster. Perhaps my faith was too small? Perhaps I was not righteous enough?

At six months old, Titus stopped growing. Then, he began shrinking in on himself until he was nothing more than a skeleton, however vivacious a skeleton he was. He began throwing up meals; his stools were gritty and undigested. I turned deeper into prayer, gathered with good saints on Thursday morning to petition the healer of Jairus's daughter.

In July, we checked into Arkansas Children's Hospital. I prayed harder. I prayed and prayed until I could pray no more. And when I reckoned Jesus had been sidetracked by some other son or daughter needing a miracle, some bleeding woman somewhere, I did the same thing I perceived God was doing: I turned my back and walked away.

I remember the mornings at Children's Hospital. There, Titus and I stood at the fifth-floor window, on a walk down the hall, watching the morning rush on the highway below. I hold this memory: his cheek framed by the feeding tube that runs up his nose and down into his intestines. His brown eyes are so large, so absorbing, against the rest of his diminutive frame, and he flashes them at a woman who gawks from the nearby nurses' station before he turns back to the broad window. Titus is unaware that he is the spectacle, and runs his finger back and forth against the glass as if to trace the path of the speeding cars. He laughs.

The gawker is a visitor, and she is loud-talking to a nurse who pores over charts.

"Ooh, he's tiny," she loud-whispers to the other. I turn and catch her squinting eyes. She straightens, smiles the awkward grin of one caught, and adds, "Cute too. How old is he?" she asks.

"He'll be one on Saturday," I answer.

"Lord!" she says, jumping backward into the nurses' station. "That boy's small!"

"I know. That's sort of why we're here." Titus weighs about as much as a sixth-month-old, though he's almost one year old.

The woman turns back to the nurse and begins to talk about her grandson. He's big, she says. "Ninety-fifth percentile in height and weight. His mama was asking me the other day what ball we should use in his one-year portraits. She said, 'Soccer?' and I said, 'Now, does he look like a soccer player to you? That boy's gonna play football.'"

The woman continues her pronouncements of her grandson's grandeur—his size, his intellect, his devilish good looks. It's an exercise in compare and contrast, though I doubt she even realizes it. The nurse has turned her attention to her charts, offers intermittent *m-hmm*s as she thumbs pages one after another.

I take hold of the pole to which Titus's IV, feeding pump, feeding bag, and tube are attached, and walk back toward our room. "Bye, honey," the woman says, oblivious to the sting of her words.

My phone rings, and though I do not recognize the number, I answer. Perhaps I'm looking for a diversion to my sudden anger, but I will not get it.

It is a churchman, who says, "I'd like to share a bit of hope with you." He shares the story of his own sick son, how he was also once wasting away. He shares how God provided miraculous salvation by way of faith.

He pauses, says, "God orchestrated everything to achieve his ultimate glory. God will bring you an answer in good time because you are a man of faith."

He means all the hope in the world, but I feel gut punched. He's wrong. I am not a man of faith these days. I've converted to a fraud. I've given up on prayer.

It is then that I realize I am speaking to a ghost, the ghost of the faith healer haunting through a well-meaning churchman. These words are a scourge.

Haven't I been faithful?

Haven't I at least done right?

If Titus passes, what does that say about faith, about my faith? What does that say about God?

The man on the line tells me to "hang on, keep faith in God. He is Titus's healer."

But I don't want to hang on. I'd kill for a sign, for a miracle doctor, for something to confirm I'm not walking alone.

"Sure. Thanks for calling," I say.

You see? I am a fraud.

In the days following, others will call, tell me that God ordained this moment in his sovereignty to bring himself glory. Their theology is painful. I cannot see my son as a pawn in God's grand glory-hoarding scheme. It is too much.

There is little comfort in the well-meaning smog of men's words. There's no vindication in their volume.

Ghosts haunt and haunt. The faith healer, the unwise word-wielders (oh, friends of Job!)—they visit me in the hospital. "With the faith of a mustard seed," one says, and another says, "This is all predestined for God's glory." The ghosts of faith healing and systematized theology all converge in that sanitized, suffocating space.

Our ghosts always seem to surface at the most inopportune times, don't they?

This is why I call my sister, who lives only a few miles from the hospital in Little Rock. This is why she smuggles in my medicine of choice.

⌐

"Even Jesus asked God why he was forsaken."

This is what my therapist tells me. Today, I feel forsaken. I feel abandoned within the hull of hollow faith, a hull haunted by ghosts, and without an escape hatch. But the therapist keeps telling me to turn in to this darkness.

"This is your cave," he said, "the interior place meant for you and God. You feel the darkness there? Go. He promises he'll go with you."

He didn't stop there.

"When you go into the dark places of your own soul, write how you feel. Describe the emotions, the sensations. And when you feel that there is no God, when you ask why he's forsaken you, don't be ashamed. Remember what I said about Jesus, how even he asked?"

This evening, I still feel lost, abandoned, left for dead or drinking, and I cannot decide which is worse. All my hinges feel caddywampus. I still feel that prayer is powerless, that it is an exercise in emptiness. I still feel alone.

"Even Jesus"—this is quite the pairing of words. Jesus asked why he'd been forsaken, but I'd never heard this from either the faith healer or the good Southern Baptist lot. I hear these words now, and somehow they are a comfort.

Lord Jesus Christ, Son of God, have mercy on me, a sinner. Please do not leave me or forsake me.

OCTOBER 14

I think back, remember when the doctors at Children's Hospital finally turned the corner with Titus.

The pediatric gastroenterologist determines that his stomach has shrunk and his esophagus is lined with eosinophils, which, as best as I understand, are white blood cells that attack his esophageal tissue. His stomach will not hold sufficient calories to keep him going much longer, they say, but suggest that it might be possible to stretch his capacity by continuous drip feedings. They institute a feeding regimen—*drip, drip, drip*—and slowly but surely, Titus takes in more food without vomiting.

After a week of stretching the capacity of his stomach, the doctors are hopeful that Titus can now be fed enough to stop his steady weight loss. Gains will not come immediately, they say, but we will be discharged and instructed on home care. Providing us with enough formula to continue the feeding regimen at home, the doctors direct us to a medical-equipment rental facility in Fayetteville so we can obtain a food pump. Before we are excused from the hospital, a nurse teaches us how to change the tube, to remove the old, and to snake the new up his nose and down into his empty belly. He suffers this about as one would suspect, writhing and crying, reaching to yank it from his nasal passages. I don't suppose I'd suffer well the running of a wiry worm up my nose and down to my belly. Some things are just unnatural.

In early August, we are released from Children's Hospital and given a follow-up appointment the next week. Titus looks like a bionic baby, the boy with the tube snaking from a mechanical pump that runs up his nose, down his esophagus, and into his belly. The pump is equal parts spoon, masticator, and deglutition.

In the months following our discharge, we endure round-the-clock feedings with Titus. He is still stick thin and his immune system is weak. He is prone to catch every passing cold or illness. Our community of friends and the elders of the church come to pray. They lay hands on my son, call him things like strong and blessed and full of life. They pray a man-sized hunger on him, and one sneaks in a word about having him come to visit her, because, of course, she knows how to put weight on a baby. They pray for growth, ask with fresher faith than I've been able to gather in some time.

These prayers and supplications tire me. After all, it is an insane person who engages in the same behavior in the hope of achieving a different outcome. I don't suppose myself insane, so instead of these spiritual gyrations, I find a way to kill any expectations.

Unlike these prayer gatherings, there is nothing awkward or stilted about gin. It brings the memories of the honey sky over the Shire River, colors of an entirely new dimension. I remember the hippos too—majestic creatures, if not territorial guardians. There was an eagle perched on a branch overhanging the river banks, and under him was the glint of a teal kingfisher. The two dove for fish as synchronized air-swimmers. They were masters of their own waters, the eagle hunting in the deep, the kingfisher in the shallower. Upon snagging their quarry, each returned to their nests, to their constituent hatchlings, before going back for seconds. They ducked and dodged, turned on a dime to avoid the crocs and hippos that regarded them, I am sure, as we might view an energetic gnat.

These animals—they were one with the Shire.

I was an outsider on the Shire, just as I am in the prayer circle, but there is something to the far shore, something to the convergence of color on the horizon. Saul said of the far shore, "That's where the elephants are. They'll come closer to the river when the dry season sets in."

My grandfather once asked me about the Shire River. I told him of the eagle and the kingfisher, of the hippos and the crocs. I told him of the lilac and honey sky. We were on the dock overlooking Bayou Desiard, and the wood ducks were lighting on the water, making their way to their box houses among the cypress groves. "I'd like to see that before I die," he said, "but I suppose I won't." Taking a deep swig of his gin and tonic, he said, "I hope you'll visit the far side of the river one day." His baritone laughter bounced from the bayou as still as black glass.

If I close my eyes, if I hold my head and my nose just so, I can smell the botanicals in the gin and I am transported back to the Shire, back to the bayou dock with my grandfather. I imagine natural beauty, the summing up of all things in the fiery clarity of an African sunset. I think of my grandfather, how he rocked me as a boy, how he promised I could slay every dragon.

There is a place of complete oneness, a whole place. There is a home place too. I know these things. For now, though, I know that this home place is not found in nostalgic notions. Romanticizing gin is an act of escapism, a chasing of shadows. The African river, my grandfather's best bottle—these are not honest places of complete peace.

In the days following Titus's release from the hospital, I used liquid solace, memories, and any other escape hatch I could find to avoid the pain of an unhealthy son and a God that seemed absent.

We all seek solace in some place.

Don't we?

Lord Jesus Christ, Son of God, have mercy on me, a sinner. Visit me in my affliction; give me a sense of oneness in you, a home in you. Do not let me escape.

OCTOBER 16

It's a blur now, the season after Titus is released from the hospital. I remember it now like the ghost of a memory.

Titus meets me at the door, arms raised. The plastic snake still runs up his nose and into his belly, though he is not connected to the feeding pump at the moment. He runs bowlegged, belly bloated, smiling straight into my arms. He is a boy with unexplainable energy considering his calorie-deficient diet. I hold him, feel his heart beating through his shell of a body. I can count every rib.

These are the days when I first notice my nerves are unraveling, fraying from the inside out, first in my stomach. I can feel an ungluing of attention. I avoid prayer like frogs or locusts, like a death angel. Instead, I slow unorganized thoughts, fear, and grief with a drink or two or three. I have become a secret imbiber, pouring doubles from my stash at the office before I leave. I pour a drink when I hit the door too, a scalding gin and tonic, always more gin than tonic. When Amber goes to the bathroom, I double back to the cupboard, grab the bottle, and top off my drink. I keep multiple kinds of liquor in the house so the emptying headspace is less noticeable.

These are the things that are the hardest to confess: I am, by nature, a sneak and a thief. I'd steal a drink sooner than I'd steal a kiss, and what's worse, I'd excuse it in the name of Christian liberty.

I tell myself it's all just petty theft; it keeps the nerves at bay. But this is gunpoint robbery. I play worship music over the house speakers and feign that the music is salve to the soul, as if I'm Saul, the playlist a harp-strumming David. But the worship is much less about personal devotion; it is a cover-up.

In the later years of his life, my grandfather practiced the discipline of crucifying Gordon and his gin for the Lenten season. He'd shelve his survival kit and drudge his way through the cycle, his temper as terse as a Bengal tiger's. "I suppose this proves I don't have a problem," he'd say after a few Sundays. Then he'd laugh and add, "Think God would mind if I took a nip, just to keep the malaria at bay?"

The mosquitos on the bayou were, after all, quite a scourge.

My grandmother, on the other hand, came clean with all the devotion of a disciple set free. In her later years, she was a principled woman, a woman who did not suffer religious artifices easily. To her, the stuff of God was real and active. It was a thing not to be invoked willy-nilly. This, I suppose, had to do with the fact that she'd have died a drunk were it not for her belief in an ever-present, always-abiding Jesus.

I could have learned a thing or two from my grandmother. After all, a drunk who's found herself sobered up by interaction with a higher power deserves a bit of extra attention. My grandmother was spiritually awakened and, for the most part, could have given two cow pies about the religious Parcheesi played by the more pious.

It was my unfortunate luck, however, not to have learned the proper lessons. If I'm honest, I judged my grandmother as something other than a saint in my younger days of faith, she with the sordid history. I suppose I thought her some sort of second-tier believer.

Now here I am. A lay worship leader, a faith writer, an editor of a website titled *Deeper Church* (how much more religious could that sound?), and I have been playing my own games with devotion.

Ah, what a false face.

This morning, I read the fourth and fifth chapters of Luke. There is Jesus. Do you see him? He is there to proclaim good news to the poor, liberty to the captives, recovery to the blind and those who are oppressed. Do you see him? There he is healing the man with the demon, healing Simon's mother-in-law (Matt. 8:14–15). There he is healing the leper and the paralytic (Matt. 8:1–3; 9:1–8). He is the cure personified.

I've been sober for almost one month, but I still feel the creeping sickness. It's hiding in me, as if under a rock. I can feel the house-burning nerves. I still crave the drink. I think about liquor less, but still often. Sometimes I consider that if a tragedy occurred—if Amber died or I lost my job—I would have the perfect excuse to turn a bottle up. Could anyone blame me? And though these fantasies of drinking myself through tragedy are abating, I still have them. There is no complete relief.

I am a man of unslaked thirsts.

Today, I decide I'm finished with feeling like a fraud. I ask for the coming of real freedom: *Liberate me! Heal me! Give me good news!*

As sure as I ask for liberation, I am swept into the cave, and I feel the flames. There is the faith healer. There is the sickly me of anemic faith. All relics that remind me that my best prayers for healing have only ever gone unanswered—at least, so it feels. My tongue burns; the heat in this house fire of a cave brings everything to a blistering point. Here is the need to see an upward trend in Titus's growth chart. Here is the reminder that the far side of the river I most hope for is wholly outside my reach.

The heat is sickening, and I want my escape hatch.

I want escape from these thoughts and from the supposed safety of drink.

This is what it means to face the pain, and if you were to ask me how I feel in the quickening moments, I'd tell you that I feel abandoned, empty, sick. I feel false, a lay minister adept at the forms and structures of a Christlike faith, but lacking in power.

There are hollow prayers I've considered not worth uttering. Today, I'll pray them.

Liberate me! Heal me! Give me good news!

At first, my requests for relief only rattle and echo in my stomach. So I ask again and I hear. What? The coming of something quiet?

Yes.

I am the Lord your God; I will never leave you nor forsake you.

I hear a smaller voice too, a younger one. I tune my ears with the faith of my five-year-old self in his mesquite sanctuary, the boy before the wrecked mechanics of a well-meaning, systematized adulthood.

He is the Lord your God. These other things—they are mirages.

Yes. I hear this fresh.

Lord Jesus Christ, Son of God, have mercy on me, a sinner. Make me unafraid to pray for healing.

PART 2
THE BENDING

how should tasting touching hearing seeing
breathing any—lifted from the no
of all nothing—human merely being
doubt unimaginable You?
(now the ears of my ears awake and
now the eyes of my eyes are opened)
—FROM E. E. CUMMINGS, "I THANK YOU
GOD FOR MOST THIS AMAZING"

In the months before my coming clean, Amber asks me whether I have considered taking a break from drinking.

"Perhaps you don't *need* to drink every day? You've had a drink every day for the last several months," she says.

"No," I say. "I didn't drink . . ." I trail off, considering the most recent forgettable day. "Last Thursday." It's a firm assertion. She looks past the lie.

"Have you considered that God might have something for you, that you might be at risk of screwing it up with your drinking? It worries me."

She is trying to tattoo me with purpose again, leave some Spirit mark on my skin. This is something I'm not ready for. I resist.

I might say I could stop whenever I like, or that I live in Christian liberty, and Christian liberty should be celebrated. I might say I write better when I drink. I might wring out every cliché in every after-school special from the 1980s, depending on the given day.

Some things aren't red flags; they're mushroom-cloud warnings. There is radiation that could blow this way if the winds shifted just so. I feel the winds shifting, but I'm a fallout kind of guy. I smile. I like mushrooms.

⌒

In the calendar week before drying out, I give myself to drinking. Amber is away, neck-deep in ministry events, and I am left to tend to a career, four boys, and a habit that's become an affair. After work, I drink on the sly, just enough to keep a gentle buzz. I cook supper and tend to the evening bathing and teeth-brushing ritual. I tuck the boys into bed at 8:00, and at 8:05 I turn up bottles with great gusto. I drink on the couch, television streaming nothing in particular. It streams a History Channel documentary about the life of Hitler, or the pilot episode of *Sherlock*. I do not care about content. I am content to drink myself to sleep for eight days.

I wake with the rhythmic head-thud of a morning mallet. My nerves are soothed, though. Coffee and aspirin begin the trick of relief. By noon, I am somewhere near clearheaded. By four, I start the process of numbing my match-lit nerves. I keep a gentle buzz until 8:05, the time at which the boys are asleep, and then I'm back at it. Bottoms up.

This rhythm doesn't feel problematic. It is only rhythmic. Sometimes rhythms are just rhythms. But sometimes problems wear pretty masquerades, dance to rhythms.

On Thursday, I'm to drive to Austin to meet Amber, who is at the tail end of a Christian women's conference. There we'll exchange cars, and she'll return to Fayetteville while I attend a different conference over the following weekend. This is part of our rhythm—ministry obligations, family logistics, a busy schedule that is convenient for hiding secrets. Wednesday night, I make a run for another bottle of gin, a replacement. I drink it to an appropriate headspace, hoping she'll not think it a new bottle. The empty bottles raise too many questions, and I'm afraid Amber might consider me an alcoholic if she returns to this container full of bottles. I gather them—one gin bottle, one whiskey bottle, a tequila bottle, and numerous beer bottles—and I load them in a garbage bag. Thursday morning, before pulling from Fayetteville, I take them to my office dumpster, pitch them in secret.

These could be the anxious acts of a guilty man always looking over his shoulder, but I sink only into the rhythm. If I feel the fire,

I quench it. This is the way of things; it's the way I reckon they'll always be—that is, if I reckon anything of it at all.

⌐——

Here is the difference between the healed of Scripture and me. I do not feel my sickness, cannot see my own blindness. Jesus' patients were eye-opened people of faith. Didn't the paralytic know he was a paralytic? Didn't the lame know he was lame? Didn't the hemorrhaging woman know she was hemorrhaging? There was the mustard seed of faith in their requests. Wasn't there always?

Except maybe there wasn't. Every rule has an exception.

The demon-possessed man of the Gerasenes—did he have his wits about him when Jesus came healing? Did he exercise extraordinary faith prior to the exorcism? There's no indication of it in Scripture.

The demoniac—maybe he is my twin brother.

I travel to Austin unaware that I have become the cave dweller, the anemic addict. I am faithless and all fired up for the numbing.

Where is my mustard seed (Matt. 17:19–20)?

OCTOBER 18

What is the truth about truth? If it is absolute, if it is not subject to interpretation, why can I not perceive it? Where does it hide? Behind the eyes and between the ears? Is it secreting away in the nooks and crannies of my brain; does it burrow down somewhere between the folds where it waits to be germinated? Is it a seed? Does the soil sometimes turn on it, refuse to give the truth a place to root down? Do synaptic thorns choke it, kill it young?

Yes. I think that's it.

Or maybe not.

Maybe there's something more to it. I read an article that indicates long-term alcohol abuse may lead to damage of the central auditory pathways in the brain, that it can lead to hearing loss. Addiction is a jealous lover. She whispers lies straight past the inner ear, straight to the auditory cortex. She dulls the ears, perhaps the inner ear too. The inner ear—this is the epicenter of balance, of upright walking. Maybe addiction upsets this too.

Addiction is a flattering lover who distracts us from the pains of the day. Yes, maybe that's it.

But not entirely.

Certain truths remain absolute, even though they are unseen. They are hidden by the hazy webs of self; addiction—isn't she a venomous spider? She spins alternative, sticky truths. Her webs occupy to the exclusion of others. She injects cravings that become needs, cravings that numb the pain of being eaten alive. I consider it, how my head was once a tangle of webs, how it still is on occasion.

My head is clear today, though. There are no lovers or webs. I consider the truth—the simple, sober *Truth*—and it is this: I drove to Austin expecting to be exposed or dried out. I drove to Austin with a festering heart. I drove to Austin under the influence of something poisonous, something other. And despite the something other that occupied my hearing, the still small whisper I first heard in my childhood mesquite grove in Texas cut through the noise, burned every gossamer thread of tangled web.

It found me, this voice of voices.

There are pains that can be numbed with addiction, and the ways of addictions are myriad: some acceptable, others secret. The ways of undoing addiction—really undoing, I think—are few: confess and kill addiction; root out the underlying pain.

Lord Jesus Christ, Son of God, have mercy on me, a sinner. Be the foot crushing the spider.

On the weekend of the coming clean—almost one month ago—I travel to Austin for a conference in which I am presenting on the topic of international adoption ethics, how worldview, international legal frameworks, and gospel dignity shape our discussion of it. This has been a pet area of my legal research over the last few years. Riveting, eh?

A group of friends from across the country meet for the conference, and we rent a house at 1900 David Street, split the room and board.

There we are, together. Chad and Sarah hail from California and hide their always-tender hearts behind an ever-playful exterior. Kristen is an expert in psychology, orphan care, fashion, and just about any other thing she sets her mind to. Karen is the literary agent's wife who nurtures a beautiful mystic spirit. John Ray and his wife, Jane, bring maturity to the group, having walked through too many pains in their one life. Matt is the strong-but-quiet type, and he fights for the rights of children with special needs. Rob is the rescuer of the trafficked. Mike is my metaphorical big brother. Preston is my metaphorical younger brother. And then there's me.

We gather under the roof of the spacious rented house under the broad-shouldered and gnarled Spanish oak. I note the Spanish oak, the way it reaches heavenward. This could be a house of praise, I think as I toss my bags on the bed and fetch a beer.

And it is. These friends—we've all taken to calling it the David House, on account of its address. This is the house after God's own heart.

In the evening, Troy and Tara, missionaries from Haiti, stop by the house, and our mutual friend Sarah is in tow. Jess stops in too, peppering the conversation with a little preconference banter about orphan reunification. Good people from around the country convene for the conference, and they come in and out of the David House, all chatting and singing and enjoying the low-key house party. I lose track of the moment, though, struggle to keep tabs on my alcohol consumption.

How many drinks can a good drinker drink and still appear to be undrunk? This is my present tongue twister.

I try to balance on the edge between sober and drunk. I shotgun a beer and take nips of whiskey until the buzz sets in, then I cycle drinks on the half hour. I interrogate myself: do I feel drunk? Will the other Christians think me drunk? Am I in control of my vocal volume? Am I grinning too much, laughing at inane jokes, giggling like a sixth grader?

On Friday night, a good lot of us sit on the porch, they sipping beers, I downing whatever I manage to pour straight into the cup. I move from room to room, offer to refill the ladies' wine glasses or to grab a beer for the brothers. I am hospitable, no? No. When hospitality is motivated by selfish desire, it's no kind of hospitality at all. I am hosting myself to another drink every time I go to the kitchen.

Around eleven I grab a tequila bottle from the cupboard and make my way to the front porch. I reach for the door, and Preston sees me, bottle in hand. "Hey!" he says, smiling. It is his tequila. I turn, give him a dismissive wave of the hand. "Nothing to see here, don't mind me," I say, opening the door. He stands as if he might intervene, as if he might rescue his liquor, but instead, he lets me go. I walk to the railing, slide against it and sit on the coarse board floor, slide the bottle behind my back, between the railing and me.

On the front porch, Karen, Mike, and a houseguest are deep in conversation. Mike is asking Karen what brings her to this convocation, this conference on human rights and human care.

Karen shares about her adopted son, how he makes her want to find justice for the many children who will never be adopted. I try to engage, but am a full sentence behind in the conversation. My attempt to enter the discussion spills across the porch. Mike looks at me, shushes me by snapping his thumb and the upper part of his hand together like a lobster claw, then laughs. "Go back to drinking," he says. He knows that I have passed the point of tipsiness.

I pour a half shot of tequila into the tiny juice glass and throw it back. There is a burn here that blurs the ears, one that mutes the volume of the porch conversation. Karen continues her story, and here am I, choosing to lose presence. Mike asks me a question. I lose his train of thought too, and they roll on, always a step ahead.

I begin to count drinks again. Will the half shot put me over the edge? I had two glasses of wine at dinner and took a break from six to seven. Then I took a double of whiskey at seven, a beer at eight. Another at eight thirty? No, I don't think I drank between eight thirty and nine. Three drinks between nine and ten thirty?

I step inside to relieve myself, and on my way back out to the porch, I ask, "Where's my beer?" It is a light-headed eleven o'clock. "You drank it," says a woman with gypsy eyes. "Maybe you don't need another?" Maybe she's right about the beer, but how could the thief in me resist the good tequila at hand?

Back on the porch, I watch as the Spanish oak twirls crooked about the yard.

Am I on the edge or am I over? Have I thrown caution to the wind? Has the wind thrown me against caution? Who cares? I indulge in another double of tequila, then another. Perhaps another? I lose track in the wee hours of the morning and crawl onto the couch sometime before the five o'clock hour. There is a bed waiting for me, but would my roommates hear me stumble in? Would they smell tequila?

This time, even I am out of rhythm. I am an embarrassment to myself.

Yes, Austin is the place where the acute point of the Spirit's voice divided me, called me to inner sobriety. These things that led me to drink—Titus's sickness, the lack of healing, the history of cessationist theology, *et cetera, et cetera*—these are just the bones of my story. These are the walking bones, the calcified facts, the skeleton of self without the Spirit essence. The truth is, the childhood sense of wonder was with me once, the Spirit present in my earliest faith.

One month later, in the sleeping house of new morning light, I heard whispers of this truth. I closed my eyes, gave myself to the quiet. I imagined my five-year-old self oohing in wonder at the wind in the mesquite trees. There was the roadrunner, enlivened by the new dawn, and the scissortail flycatcher, diving on insects in midflight. This was my Father's house, and his presence was at play in the world around me. I heard my younger laughter in the whistling of the winds in the short, crooked tree arms.

The child is who I am. He is who I've always been. But as I sit in the quiet, as I plumb the interior places of my heart, I find the stick-thin me (oh me of little faith!) and the taunting faith healer with the silken pocket square. Their memory is at odds with childlike faith, and they cast shadows of doubt. Did God really dance with me in the mesquite trees? Did his breath animate the roadrunner and flycatcher? This morning, though, I consider the truth and see these inner apparitions of addict and preacher for who they are: sick men who've both lost their essence. They are the disembodied pains that underlie my habit, and the liquor lulls them to silence.

We begin this life in unity with God. Along the way, though, a mitosis happens, a division of essence from self. You, me, the faith healer—we all separate ourselves from simple faith at some point.

These days, I'm praying for fusion. I'm praying for a unification of my present self and the essence of childhood belief. I am looking for an inner sanctuary unspoiled by mocking voices. I'm looking for an interior space reserved for the presence of God, which sweeps in like a mesquite wind and casts out all fear and disbelief. Is such a thing possible?

Maybe these thoughts are too disorganized for your liking. This journal comprises, after all, a swirl of memories and metaphors. The place of my childhood calling from which I seem separated, the inner cave where the sick man and the faith healer haunt, the child me whispering—is there a point here?

Disorganized? Yes. If pain took an organized, nameable, tangible, physical shape, it'd be an easy thing to put to death. It turns out, though, that to beat the shame out of you, you have to give the pain in your life contours. At least, that's what my therapist says.

I'm finding the way around my contours here. Maybe you could start finding your way around your own contours? Are you burying your pain? Are you numbing it with your own vices?

This is not a clean story. This is a story of coming clean.

OCTOBER 21

I had a dream about my grandmother last night.

The family was there, all of us at the old home place overlooking the cypress-shaded bayou banks. I was sitting at the family dining table on the back porch when my mother up and announced to anyone within earshot that "Seth is an alcoholic, so please do not hoist a millstone around his neck by offering him a drink." She said this, of course, holding a red Solo cup that smelled of lime and gin. I lashed out, told her it wasn't her story to tell, that I'd rather share my story in my own way.

"Let me raise my own Ebenezers," I said.

She blushed, apologized for the production, and made her way to the back shadows of the kitchen. Even in dreams, I have developed ways of holding people at arm's length.

My grandmother appeared at the table, sitting next to me, her sad blue eyes welling with tears. She was wearing a stern, kind smile. I'd seen this look before; it was her "I agreed to sponsor so-and-so in their twelve-step program" face. She reached from the head of the table to my isolated corner. She said, "I'm so proud of you, Seth. This is all going to work just fine. You watch."

That was it. I woke warm.

What are dreams? Are they composed of magic, or of unpacked memories? Are they full of the thoughts of men, or of the echoes of souls departed?

Some psychologists claim that dreams are our attempt to organize junked-up thoughts. We recycle the useful, catalog it; we scrap the usable iron, send the rest to rust in the rain. Dreams are the winnowing fork, the way we separate wheat from chaff. At least, this is what the noggin doctors say, and I know this must be true, because the letters after their names evidence their expertise in noggin doctory.

Maybe the nogginologists are right. But what if dreams are more?

In this life, we leave our marks on those around us. Perhaps some of those marks run more like record grooves. Suppose we can put a needle in the grooves; suppose we can play the best part of each other by way of dreams. Suppose my dream was a recording set for me long ago by my grandmother; suppose she left me this word for a day when I'd need it.

My grandmother is with Jesus, she a firm believer. Suppose the Spirit told her the right words to say so that I'd recall them at the moment I'd need them most. In that way, maybe my grandmother reached ahead of the grave, gave me the peace that, yes, it's going to be okay. I'll see. And she'll be proud.

This is the believing.

It's all going to be okay.

Lord Jesus Christ, Son of God, have mercy on me, a sinner. May I hear the better wisdom of my grandmother.

Here, I'll show you the anatomy of an undoing.

Drink yourself to sleep for eight days straight. Drink at the first inkling of doubt, of pain, of upendedness. Drink until you feel like a slave to the couch. Drive to Austin and shack up in the company of good Christian people; occupy yourself with alcoholic mathematics; count drinks for two days while others around you are sharing life; try your best to get ahead of conversations, to catch yourself before you utter the drunk stupid thing that seems so brilliant in the moment; sit against the rails on the front porch with a bottle of tequila in the small of your back; wake late on the third day and rely on Tsh to bring you to the conference venue; hope she doesn't smell tequila on your breath when you thank her for the breakfast tacos she's brought, because she is among the circle of people who might catch the stiff scent of hypocrisy like a coyote does roadkill.

I breathe out of the side of my mouth, and we enter the Methodist church together. We are latecomers, and the morning speakers have already taken center stage. Before I make it through the lobby, though, I meet a prophetess.

Heather King is a new transplant to Austin, a born-and-bred Minnesotan who carpetbagged to the Lone Star State with her husband, children, and accent in tow. I've known Heather for years, she being a writer who swims in the same streams as I. Years ago, Heather wrote about her own bout with alcoholism, wrote about her process of finding sobriety. She served as inspiration for more than one sobriety story, and yet I never expected she would serve as any sort of catalyst for mine.

She approaches from the far side of the foyer on that throbbing Saturday morning, her eyes the shape of my grandmother's, her smile echoing that same grace. She turns her head sideways, asks, "How'd you sleep?"

If a man's lucky, he gets a shining moment of clarity, a veil-splitting moment. This is mine. Before I can lasso my words and tug them back, they escape into the Austin Methodist foyer, bronco-wild. I am the most accomplished Christian fraud, yes. But this time, I am caught on the very threshold, before I can ever enter the sanctuary.

"How did you know you had a drinking problem?" I ask without context.

"Oh, Seth," she says. "You know, don't you?"

I've described it since as a moment of one thousand epiphanies. The corners of the room pull taut, the ceiling lifts, the floor drops, and Heather speaks the truest question I've heard in a long time.

There's no voice from heaven, no fanfare or bright light, but the familiar Spirit-whisper is unmistakable. "You can take care of this now, or not," I hear, "but if you don't, it's downhill from here."

There I am standing in the vertigo induced by human confession, and I search for the words to put it all in perspective, to justify it all. But Heather's eyes are too much like my grandmother's, and she won't let me run.

"I've not hit my wife or my kids," I say. "I've not lost my job."

"You know that doesn't matter, right?"

"No, I don't. I was actually hoping you'd say that means I can't have a problem."

"How many drinks do you have per night?"

"What do you mean? I suppose it depends on the pour."

"Yeah, I suppose. Do you lie to Amber about it?"

"Do I lie? I don't necessarily tell the truth, and she doesn't necessarily ask," I say. "I snag a drink at around four most days. I grab a drink as soon as I get home so she'll think the smell of liquor is fresh, so she won't suspect me of drinking at the office. I top off drinks when she goes to the bathroom. I use too much liquor in my mixed drinks. But lie?"

Her slight frame straightens. "I'm sorry. I can't tell you whether you have a problem, but you know, right? In your heart of hearts, you know?"

She is pushing into truth with only questions.

This is the beginning of an awakening, the genesis of one thousand epiphanies. I couldn't stop them if I tried. "Now what?" I ask Heather.

"It sounds cliché, but it's the best I have," she says, and then adds, "You have to take it one day at a time. This is day one."

Later, we meet the housemates on the front steps of the church for lunch. We walk the streets of downtown Austin looking for some quaint lunch dive that doesn't peddle food from an Airstream window. While the others forge ahead discussing the morning sessions together, Heather and I lag back, talk in lower tones about dependency and addiction. She keeps me in the tension, won't allow me to turn the conversation into convenient excuses. Then again, I don't really want to.

She tells me her story, and it sounds too familiar. She tells a story of a sick child. She tells a story of nervous energy, of anxiety, of unstoppable feelings. It sounds like my grandmother, the escape artist. It sounds like my uncle too. (He was, they say, a raging bull of an alcoholic.) It sounds like my burning, like my unhinged desire for something less Spirit led and more led by the spirits. It sounds like kin, like me.

In this conversation, I see myself in earnest. I am the Spirit avoider, the feeling number who does not want to consider the sickness of his son any longer. I see the liar, the Adam who in his shame avoids his evening walk with God. I see the truest me, the self-medicator, the mathematician who counts shots instead of remaining present; I am the secret emptier of all the best tequila bottles. I am these very empty people and not the Christ-filled man I'd rather be.

I barely remember the wind in the Texas mesquite trees, but the Austin humidity is raising memories like Christ raised Lazarus. There was a time when I heard the God of one thousand epiphanies, plain and sure. Was I a child? Yes. But I know what I heard. It is September 21, and I am hearing it again. He spoke in the still small whisper, and he did it through a woman who shares the eyes of my grandmother.

"I have never left nor forsaken you. There is healing if you let there be," he says.

In that moment, Heather is a conduit for the Spirit of God. I'll not soon take these words back.

———

This journaling is a hodgepodge, a mishmash of thoughts as they come. It is a stream-of-consciousness whirlwind, maybe, but I've been fighting for a thread running through. I'm finding the thread, tugging it free.

I have a friend, a good friend, who described the awakening from the alcoholic haze as a tornado of mental activity. It's a swift, disorganized wreck of a storm. There are quite sudden and very real pains that must be accounted for. These pains flood in from all directions, and on some evenings, that feels truer than others. This is one of those truer evenings.

I'm sitting with my journal in bed and remembering Austin. Amber reads a book beside me, glasses on and looking studious in her pajamas. We'll talk about my journaling before we turn the lights out, but for now, she's engrossed in another world. From time to time, she reaches out and rubs my arm. This is her silent encouragement to keep doing the interior work. This is her way of saying she is with me.

The pain, it seems, is easier to count on than the prayer. And this is mine: I've been sitting with Titus's sickness and the lack of a healing, and asking an abiding God to come near.

"How does it feel? The emotion, that is," my therapist asked me this afternoon.

The question brought me to the darker places of the cave. There was tingling, shortness of breath, numbness in my fingertips, I said. I described the feelings, and they manifested on command.

"Do you feel it now?" he asked.

"Oh boy, do I," I blurted.

"Good, let's go with that. Describe the emotions."

"I feel alone, hopeless. Maybe like a fraud. I'm supposed to know the truth of a present God, and in these moments I feel a sense of intense lostness." I closed my eyes, felt the velvet blanket folding over me, covering my eyes, leaving no space for light breaking through. The velvet blanket came first, then the sense of cawing passerine birds descending in a murder, their voices unraveling my nerves. My skin prickled as if being pecked apart.

This is how I felt.

"Are you afraid?" he asked.

"Of what?"

He typed a note in his laptop. "If you aren't afraid, then what are you?"

"I don't know how to say this—and please hear what I'm saying—I don't want to kill myself, but sometimes I wish it were all over. I don't feel like there's any relief from all the sickness. I don't feel like there's anything real and whole here. Maybe I'd like to stretch into the other side and see whether it gets made right. Maybe I'd like to see if there is any healing from all this."

He considered my comment, responded, "You know this is not uncommon, right?" His question sent a wild, almost shameful shot of hope running through me.

"No?" I asked.

"You're the fourth person to say this to me in the last week."

The thought brought easier breathing, but only for a moment. The smile of relief seemed sadistic, so I bit the inside of my lips.

"So let's ask God some questions about this and listen. Let's see what he says about it all."

This, of course, sounded a lot like the charismatic notions of my youth, the sitting and waiting for the magical voice of God. My skin chilled at the thought of having my faith put on the spot again.

"No pressure," he said.

"Sure," I mustered, but the pit in my stomach was opening up, splitting wide like a fissure running from a fault. My nerves started to fold, shrink away.

"Tell me what you hear, and if it's nothing, or if it's only your own thoughts, no big deal. We'll distinguish voices later. Let's start."

He bowed his head, asked God to show me the first time I felt this sense of empty loneliness, the first time I felt the resolve to see what is on the other side of living. I did not tell him, but this was a question I didn't need the Holy Spirit to answer. I remembered the closeness of God in those Texas fields. I remembered the wonder and excitement in the dancing of nature. I remembered the rumble of thunder like the coming of chariots, the flashing of lightning like the word that spoke the world into being, the rain that came blowing across the plains in a wall of grace. I remembered these things, how God spoke to me: *I am big; I have power; I can quench your thirst.*

Then I remembered the faith healer.

He broke the silence. "It was the healer? Right?"

"Yes," I said. "Before that, my experiences with God were so visceral. But after, I felt like maybe my faith wasn't good enough. I felt like I was straining toward a God who was distant at best, or who wasn't there at all."

"Let's go there," he said, and he launched into an impromptu prayer in which he asked God to reveal the truth of my childhood. That's when I heard the still small voice say it for the first time.

Go back to the mesquite trees.

I tried clearing my thoughts, and I reckoned it as only the ramblings of a unhinged mind.

Go back to the mesquite trees.

"What do you hear?"

"Go back to the mesquite trees," I said.

"Do you feel like God is taking you back somewhere?"

"No, it's more like he's sending me."

Clouded scenes from memory came into focus. There I was, a boy with windswept hair. I had lost something of great worth.

"It's like I've lost a treasured coin. That coin is the essence of who I am. He is sending me back to the mesquite trees to find it."

I was sobbing, and I realized the dirty truth: I'd lost the essence of who I was at the altar with the faith healer. He had put the onus on *me*, had put my faith on the spot, and when my mustard seed didn't transform into the tree of life, it turned into a cannonball that blew my young faith to smithereens.

For thirty years, I have held fast to this memory. For thirty years, I've been angry with the healer who harmed instead. For thirty years, I have not forgiven him.

I hear the gentle whisper—*it's time to forgive*—but I do not tell this to my therapist. It's not time yet, I don't think.

"The mesquite trees are the last place I had the faith of a child," I said. "I want to go back there."

Over the last few days, I haven't thought so much about alcohol. Sure, I was not a lunatic of a drunk; I had not been a binge drinker for fifteen years. Nonetheless, I will record it this way: I can feel the coming of the desire, and if I stop, if I pray something simple like "Lord Jesus Christ, Son of God, have mercy on me, a sinner,"

I can sense relief. And if I turn in to the anxiety that brings the drinking need, if I name it (I am counting Titus's ribs again, for instance), if I confess the feeling (hopelessness, for instance), if I release it to God and ask him to fill the empty space, then there is a quiet, small peace. Some might call it serenity. This is the hope that I might find the Spirit of those mesquite trees again.

Lord Jesus Christ, Son of God, have mercy on me, a sinner. Go with me back to the mesquite trees.

I read the words of Jesus. "Whoever wants to be my disciple," he said (and still says), "must deny themselves and take up their cross daily and follow me" (Luke 9:23). This Scripture is a clarifying voice calling.

There are, of course, various responses to any voice, including the still small voice. I suppose the many potential responses—the yes, the no, the maybe, the everything in between—mingle somewhere within the place we call the human will. The will—is this the part of humanity that must be mastered? Is this the *I* that must be "crucified with Christ" so that "it is no longer *I* who live"? The will, though—isn't it most persistent, most vicious, the most dogged in its pursuits?

As I see it, the crucifixion of the will feels less like a crucifixion and more like a drowning. Perhaps this is because I've never taken up a cross; I've never been crucified, and don't plan on being anytime soon. I've never seen a crucifixion either (I avoided watching Mel Gibson's film *The Passion of the Christ* because I could not stand to watch such graphic torture), and I don't suppose I'll happen upon the infamous form of Roman torture anytime soon. My hands have never been pierced through, and I've never worn a crown of thorns. I have been impaled by my fair share of Texan field stickers, but I don't suppose this to be even the remotest of corollaries.

No, I've never been crucified, but I know well the sensation of sinking. I was with my father when our canoe capsized in the icy spring waters of the Buffalo River, and though my feet could touch the bottom even as a boy, the needling waters robbed me of any semblance of orientation.

Yes, I think killing the worst part of the will, the part that refuses to listen to the voice of God, feels less like a crucifixion and more like the sinking of your own ship.

Every time I consider releasing addictions—that infernal everyday occurrence—a familiar capsizing dread creeps in, and with it the skin prickle of the cold Buffalo waters. These thoughts of coming clean steal our breath, don't they?

Perhaps you might say, "Seth, you are describing nothing more than common anxiety and mild panic." Allow me to respond: I find nothing common about either anxiety or panic. You might tell me anxiety and panic can be mastered by stopping, breathing, relaxing, and the like. I'd prefer to treat it with a Xanax and a chaser of whiskey. In any event, doesn't every well-meaning person panic when their canoe is capsizing or being weighed down by too much water?

Addiction is a canoe on the Pacific. It may keep you afloat for a while, but at some point, you're bound to be overturned. And if there were a luxury cruise liner nearby, wouldn't you abandon ship? Wouldn't you brave the icy waters for more secure and better appointed passage?

I don't know about you, but I'm sinking my canoe in favor of a bigger, better vessel. And even if I find myself resurrected each morning in the hull of that tiny boat, I'll commit it to sinking again; I will brave the icy waters for the better boat. And perhaps again. And perhaps again.

Yes, it is a daily decision to sink the old will, a decision I'm often too spent, too water-disoriented, to make.

But just when I think I can no longer sink my ship for the umpteenth time, I send up the distress call, and here comes the God of rescue. He drags me from my vices and turns the howitzer on that smallest canoe, shows me how futile the vessels of my making are.

The Bending

Lord, Jesus Christ, Son of God, have mercy on me, a sinner.
Drown my will and bring peace to the war on the sea.

My first ship-sinking opportunity came on September 21 in an Austin Tex-Mex joint. Hours after my conversation with Heather, the David House occupants, along with a few tagalongs, gather at the insistence of my friend John Ray, who has spent the better part of his formative years in Austin. A pastor now, John hopes to revisit his more innocent days through the comfort food of his youth.

We descend on El Patio like ants on a lollipop, more than twenty of us. The waitstaff tells us we are no trouble, but they are only being polite. My waiter asks me if I'd like a drink, at which point that infernal internal war begins.

In moments of fresh epiphany, it's easy to write off inklings and unctions. When the sense of conviction comes, the will wages war, says, "It's just my emotions talking," or, "Was that *really* God's voice, or was it mine?" The will whispers things like, "You can have a drink. You can stop at one."

This, I think, is the age-old question of the serpent in Genesis: "Did God really say?" There truly is a devil on our shoulders.

Heather is at the far end of the table, and she alone knows I am struggling with the drink. I have not yet made any sort of confession to any other. There is a creeping tension between us. Maybe she's watching to see what I order? Maybe this is a test of my commitment? Of my will?

"Water," I tell the waiter. This is the first little victory, the first drowning of desire.

My friends do not notice I'm drinking water, and they turn up bottles of beer and lick the rims of salted margarita glasses. I notice every beverage raised, even the fruity frozen ones.

Leaving the restaurant, Heather catches me. "I hope you didn't order water on my account," she says. She noticed. "There's no judgment here, you know. There's no shame."

"I know. I'm pretty sure I have to quit altogether, though. It's day one, right?"

The confession feels awkward, unnatural. It is the second little victory.

Water rushes over wood with the confession, and the ship sinks.

The lot of us returns to the David House, and I pull John and Matt aside, confess that comfort food isn't my bag. I have chosen the bottle instead. I confess I need to quit, ask them to help keep me away from the drinks of the David House. This is little victory number three, the confession and cry for help that sinks a night's worth of ships.

John asks whether I've called Amber, whether I've confessed it yet, and the truth is I don't want to. "You should probably take care of that, right?" he asks.

I dial the number and she answers the phone.

"I think I need you to get rid of all the alcohol in the house," I tell her. "I think I have to quit drinking."

"You have a drinking problem?" she asks, and as the words hang, I cannot respond.

"Yes," I manage after too long a pause.

"Okay," she says. "I love you."

This is my fourth little victory. Or maybe it's not little at all.

―――――

My friends in Austin taught me it takes a village to break through to freedom. These cycles of addiction (no matter the addiction), the breaking of them—it's tricky business. When I'm sober-minded, anxiety lurks, doubts nag, the ghosts beckon. When I'm sober-minded, the contours of life are more angular, the textures rougher. When I'm sober-minded, I'm left with my thoughts and nerves in full, unfiltered function, and perhaps this is just a bit about my personality, but my thoughts are sometimes rather unpleasant and my nerves are ever on edge.

When I'm sober-minded, though, I hear the wisdom of my community and can lean on its strength. I can muster the courage to drink water or call my wife or be honest about my dependency.

When I'm sober-minded, I can also hear the truth of the Spirit—*I am a self-medicator; this moment is painful; self-medicating with alcohol squeezes the still small voice from the mind.* When I'm sober-minded, Scripture comes alive. When I'm sober-minded, I can pray for healing, difficult though it still is. I can pray for the drowning of the will, the sinking of the ship of desire. When I'm sober-minded, I have the heightened chance to stay sober-minded.

Yes, this is the way it works. Is your bag liquor? Is it porn or cakes or puking? Is your bag status or style, theological or intellectual prowess? Are you addicted to the notion that you have some modicum of power or money or fame? Does your dependency or addiction isolate you from community or the still small voice of God? Are you really sober-minded? Are you willing and able to sink your ship, to drown your destructive will and answer the call of one who loves?

Last night, I attended parent-teacher conferences at my children's school. Mrs. Wingo slid an essay across the table to me. It was written by my secondborn, Jude. Mrs. Wingo had asked her first graders to write about an awkward experience and to include a beginning, a middle, and an end to the story. As it is, Jude comes from a long line of storytellers and is well acquainted with the idea of narrative arc, even at only seven years old.

"Jude did very well on his essay. He wrote about a dream he had, which he said was awkward. He was able to write a beginning, middle, and ending."

His essay read something like this (with corrected spelling, punctuation, and such): "I had a dream. My dream was awkward. We were playing and everyone got a disease. Everyone with the disease melted into a puddle, but they didn't die. They were talking puddles. There was no medicine, so they stayed puddles. I tried to help them, but then I woke up. It was not a scary dream. It was funny to see my friends as talking and laughing puddles." I wonder whether I'm one of Jude's puddled-up friends; after all, along the way I lost my shape.

This morning, Isaac came into the living room, sat on the couch, and rubbed his crusty eyes. "Daddy," he said, "last night I dreamed about math problems all night. When I woke, I caught myself saying 'six times four is twenty-four' over and over."

There are truths hidden in the dreams of the young. Maybe some of us, by giving in to the disease of all humanity, poison ourselves, allow ourselves to melt and puddle up on the ground. Maybe the way out, the path to wisdom, is to obsess on the truth, to recite it so much that it occupies the spaces of our sleeping. Perhaps this is what the psalmist meant when he said, "I have hidden your word in my heart, that I might not sin against you" (Ps. 119:11).

This constant dwelling on the truth—it is more than calcifying; it is skeletal steel. The truth, I think, gives us the ability to face the rougher edges, the sharper contours. And this brings me to the meat of the matter: the liquor keeps me from dealing with the pain I have hidden in the cave of my soul. The liquor makes me a coward, keeps me from hearing the voices in the darker places of the soul-cave. The liquor-hiding isolates me from the community of faith that helps hold me up. This is the way of any addiction, isn't it? Aren't all of our vices just a convenient distraction from the voice of God speaking to the inner person, from his community that speaks too?

There are diseases that keep us from being fully formed; they puddle us up on every floor. Are you sick with one?

OCTOBER 25

It is my birthday. Today, I turn thirty-six.

My grandfather used to say he felt always eighteen behind the eyes. Perhaps he was saying only that he maintained his sense of childish wonder. Perhaps he was alluding to the fact that he never saw the shape of a woman he didn't rather enjoy. Perhaps, though, he was saying something more. Perhaps it was his subtle way of recognizing the ego, recognizing how the stubborn pride of adolescence forever stunts maturity, or at least is a reminder of the never-refined parts of us.

I am thirty-six, and I wonder if I'm only now stumbling into the wisdom of adulthood. I still feel eighteen behind the eyes.

———

Heather sent me happy birthday wishes today, speaking her signature quiet kind of truth. The message read, "Happy Birthday, Mr. Seth. It's kind of cool how we get to be born so many times in life. It probably doesn't feel like it at all, but you just recently got born. Like a month ago. So many birthdays, so much living to do. It's exhausting, but you are terribly worth it. Peace."

It *is* exhausting, I think; she is right. I do feel as if I am newreborn. Just as much, I feel recently killed too. I write Heather my thanks, adding, "It's so awkward to be a phoenix."

It's the only way I know how to describe this last month. Every day a new death, a new ship to sink.

Lord, I'm tired of this kind of daily dying, the daily dying of

*the will. I'm not like the others, though, the ones who can control
the drink. The sicker parts of me love it too much.*

So I die and die and die; I sink and sink and sink the will.
My survival tactics vary day to day. Sometimes I white-knuckle
through. Sometimes I pray. *Lord, when will these growing pains
cease?* Sometimes I listen to good tunes, let the vibes sink deep. But
every day, I die anew. I live a phoenix's flaming calendar.

I wonder, do you know the phoenix of myth which, from time
to time, combusts only to rise more beautiful from its own ashes?
It is the embodiment of the cycles of life: the setting and rising sun,
the falling and rising of empires, death and resurrection. It is a bird
of metamorphosis, of transition, and of ultimate transcendence.

The phoenix is no biblical creature, but could he be a type and
shadow? Can't all metaphors be?

Death is not the whole story for the phoenix. There is an eternal new rising. But for there to be phoenix risings, there must first
come the death of the drab.

I've been practicing the daily death to my desire to drink. So
when does the rebirth happen? When the metamorphosis? When
does the weak man take heart in the voice of God's calling, allow
it to invade, to take shape, to give purpose? There has to be a resurrection moment.

Maybe today? It is, after all, my birthday.

Erika, our punk-hippie friend from Connecticut, sent me a text
message today wishing me a happy birthday. She is unafraid, a
wild, free-spirited work of art. She asked what I thought of the
new charismatics, those people who walk so in tune with the mystic whispers of God that they see no distinction between life and
communion with the Eternal. I mulled over the word charismatic.
I don't remember a time when this word didn't raise every red
flag. These were the people who prayed for healings and signs and

wonders. These were the people who ever and always asked me to put faith to the test. These were the people who tried to cram down my best life.

The word charismatic reminded me of the faith healer and sparked anxiety. So when I read her text, the familiar dark spiral set in. I stopped in the spiral, examined the anxiety with honest eyes, listened with honest ears. These were the questions.

What if there is no healing? What does that say of faith—is it too weak a thing? If it is too weak a thing, whose voice do I hear between my ears? Is this the voice of the Spirit or the wanderings of my own crazy, spinning consciousness?

I decided this will not be the day I give in to anxious thoughts, nor will it be the day I give in to the craving for gin. This is my birthday, the day of being born again. So I listened to the questions and refused to own the anxious lies. Instead, I turned to my now-familiar prayer. *Lord Jesus Christ, Son of God, have mercy on me, a sinner. Help my unbelief.*

This is where the clarity comes. The new charismatics—yes. Perhaps that term is laced with negative implications for some? Perhaps for me? But what if it's just a way of owning Jesus' promise? "Surely I am with you always, to the very end of the age," he said (Matt. 28:20). He is eternal and present. I'm going with that.

There will always be lies whispered about new birth. We can own them or not. Today, I chose not.

It's all fine and sometimes good to say we can rise like phoenixes or saints, or that we can stand against the death spiral of panic. The truth is these are platitudes that might help to calcify the will in some moments, but only for a moment.

If I'm going to rise resplendent, how? If I'm going to master the darker places of the cave—the faith healer, my gaunt doppelganger—then how? If I'm going to see God as ever present, as active in all, then I must make a shift. How does one murder the fickle fear that keeps us bound?

If I listen closely, I hear it.

Go back to the mesquite trees; go back and find the childlike faith, the mustard seed that was never given the chance to grow. Find the essence of things, your once unscarred, untainted faith.

OCTOBER 27

Saturday evening I sat on John Ray's back porch.It is, by a wide margin, my favorite place in Fayetteville. On it he keeps a well-stoked fire pit and a collection of many of Fayetteville's finest personalities. There is always Belgian beer, that flowery, yeasty stuff; it's not my favorite. On occasion, John brings an assortment of craft India pale ales. There is always wine for the women.

I was with the men, each beer-handed, and it was only a slight temptation. The ladies arrived after a time, and they came to the porch with their wine glasses. I smelled the merlot wafting across the porch, the intoxicating perfume. It was an instant temptation.

I left the porch, meandered to the kitchen to let the urge blow over. I listened to Patty Griffin crooning over John's sound system. I spoke with his wife, Jane, she chopping celery for a creamy dip. I prayed under my breath and the urge passed.

The urges—they do blow over if you give them time.

OCTOBER 28

The Monday therapy carnival continued today with a curious announcement.

Perhaps, he said, I would not have to give up alcohol forever. I told him I found this to be a dubious claim. He chuckled, said I know myself better than he, but those who are required to give up the bottle forever are those who will not go into and deal with their pain.

"If you deal with your pain, you won't need the numbness. You can stop after two drinks."

"But why would I stop at two drinks when I could keep going and feel nothing?"

"Because you're not thirsty after one or two."

I was shocked by this. Isn't alcoholism for life? Isn't that what all the experts say?

This is all a bit premature, he said, and we get back to talking about the mesquite trees. It all goes back to the mesquite trees, doesn't it?

I informed him I'd been listening to the still small voice of God the best I know how and that I've traced a line back through history and found the seed of doubt. I gathered my gumption, took a deep breath, and explained.

"There are lost pieces of my essence along the way—stolen pieces, really," I said. "I feel like my faith was manipulated, stolen. As much as it embitters me, I keep thinking about needing to extend forgiveness to that faith healer."

He stopped me.

"Before you even get to forgiveness, though," he said, "you have to sort out the source of your pain. Let's start with the faith healer," he said, which I reckoned to be a terrible place to start because the room seemed to shift and spin on an invisible axis running through the middle of my stomach. We went back anyway, back to the charismatic church, back to the anointing oil, back to my younger days of faith.

There is trauma there, yes. I told him this, told him there has always been an undercurrent of pain in my childhood church experience. I unpacked my continuing sickness, told him how I continued to struggle with asthma well after the healing service, even into my adult years. "I cannot sleep without an inhaler by my bed," I told him.

The sickness has undermined my faith, and I know this is why the prayers for Titus's healing make it no farther than the ceiling. I do not believe. Why pray for healing to the God who has ceased with the working of miracles, the God who has never quite come through on that front? Fidelity? Fortitude? Grace? These are acceptable things for which to pray. But requests for healing? You might as well sow your back yard with Corn Pops and hope to reap a harvest in due season.

"You're in a perpetual loop," he said. "It's a dangerous place."

I asked him what he means, and he said I need healing down deep. Titus still needs healing too, he said. "But," he said, "the very thing you need is the source of your pain. This isn't really about the faith healer as much as it is about healing. You consider the notion of healing, and your thoughts become unorganized; you've tried to systematize God, tried to figure why he hasn't healed you or Titus. But the notion of healing is a mystery. It's outside your systematized box. This is why thoughts of healing cause you deep anxiety. You can't control mystery."

My breath drew short, and my fingers tapped a fidgety rhythm on my knees. I've put structures in place to avoid dealing with more mystical, unpredictable things. I've tried to make God a predictable fellow. By nine, I was memorizing Scripture, learning the apologetics of good Christian thought, systematizing faith. I was taught that God had stopped with the signs and wonders bit, at least for the most part, because the perfect (the Word of God) had come, and so the imperfect (signs and wonders) had passed (1 Cor. 13:10).

In my teens, I was drawn to free-spirited believers, the ones who seemed to float on the wind, and at the same time, I pushed hard against them, thinking their belief in a miraculous, healing God to be futile at best, and weird, if I'm honest. I learned every neo-Reformed argument under the sun, reasoned that God had set things in motion, predestined everything for success or failure. My therapist knows this.

"You have systematically removed the Spirit of God from your life by building structures for him. By way of theology, you have explained away his ability to enter into your life in any meaningful way. You have created structures. Do you know what that's called?"

The question hung, and he said, "Idolatry. You've made an idol out of believing and acting the way a certain kind of Christian should. You've believed God stopped intervening in the lives of men. Can't you feel the tension, the pain in that?"

"Yes," I said, remembering leading Easter worship with a false face and a hidden hangover. "I wonder whether people will find me out." I chuckled to lighten the tension. He didn't crack a smile.

"This is normal for people who deal with any kind of trauma or manipulation of faith," he said. "You suffered the loss of your childlike faith when you were a kid, and Titus is a constant reminder of it. The childhood wonder of faith was stolen, and you think God has abandoned you. The feeling of God abandonment is too much pain for one man to take. You're lucky you started coming to grips with this before you became an atheist."

An atheist? Now there's a thought. It would make all of this much more explainable, how the grand evolutionary process spits us into existence and leaves some of us to live and all of us to die. Perhaps God is nothing more than a chemical delusion? Maybe he's the voice of my own consciousness?

"Take a minute and ask yourself whether God ever tried to get your attention, whether you've seen him work outside of tidy theological understandings."

I remembered my experience in the mesquite trees. I considered God's nearness in nature, how I see him in the trout leaping upward, how the soul rises with it, turns upward to God too. I considered how I've seen God in community, how there is a thick bond in the prayer-filled gathering of believers. There is the light of Amber's eyes when she prays, the same light that was in my grandmother who came clean under the weight of new glory. I wonder at the truly penitent, the men and women who've come to humble walking out of quiet faith without the benefit of perfect theological insight. I considered the God I have seen emerging from other Christian traditions, both charismatic and the more stolid ones.

God attempted to intervene, to show himself as present within the human experience on more than one occasion. He tried to break through the doctrinal idolatry, to remind me that he meets with the broken, the outsiders, in the everyday mundane. I consider Erika Morrison's new charismatics. For a fleeting moment, I considered Father Jack.

———

After years in the Baptist Church, my father decided to trade in his low-church evangelicalism for a more liturgical setting. He joined the Catholic Church, where folks seemed less judgmental of red wine and Crosby, Stills, and Nash records. Though we continued to attend church with my mother, my sister and I were enrolled in Catholic school when I was in the fourth grade on account of the quality of education. So I began attending Mass on a weekly basis, began the process of being immersed in a faith that did not speak my native faith tongue. I learned to cross myself, to recite the Hail Mary, to respond to Monsignor's prompting during the Mass. I learned to avoid eye contact with Sister Sarto, the Irish nun with a temper like a Roman Catholic candle. I also learned the way of being an outsider. I was not to sully the holy water with my Protestant fingers, was not to kneel in prayer prior to the start of Mass, and above all, I was not to enter the Eucharist line.

During my eighth grade year, Father Jack took on the daunting task of teaching the first-period, all-boys religion class. It was predestined by Father Jack that we should suffer through the book of Luke together. This, he said, would teach us to experience Jesus' love through the eyes of the poor and broken. It was his favorite book of the Bible, he said, to which he had given two nicknames: the Gospel of the Underdog, and the Gospel of Equality. I don't suppose I realized just how progressive all of this sounded at the time. How could I have? After all, the class was not composed of underdog sorts. Instead, the 8:00 a.m. religion class seated twenty doe-eyed, middle-class kids, most of whom were clean-cut and destined for middle management in corporate America.

Through the gospel of Luke, he taught us how Jesus reached out to women, children, and Gentiles. Father spent multiple classes on the healing of the Gerasenian demoniac and Jairus's daughter, both Gentiles. He taught with such compassion of the hemorrhaging woman, the social outcast who had sneaked into the city for a chance at healing. Jesus was always present with the sick, and by extension, he taught, we were too.

I don't remember his exact words, the particularities of his lectures, but Father Jack taught us something significant of the gospel. He taught that the mystery of Jesus' ministry was that he could have come and fixed everything all at once; he could have come to rule over a perfect and happy world. He could have overthrown Rome along with the ruling Jews. But he didn't. He came and lived among the sick, the weak, the Gentiles. His ministry was not for those who had it all together.

Father Jack's teaching could have been enough to help me see God's abiding presence with the broken outsider, with the sick who had nothing left to lose. But that year, he put his teaching into practice, allowing the Protestant students to join the Eucharist during our informal school Masses, which were held in a spacious classroom instead of the chapel. He invited the Protestants to the table, included the modern-day Gentiles in the rites of the church. I always suspected this had something to do with the fact that the services were not formally sanctioned Catholic Masses, but as I've grown older, as I've thought through Father Jack's teachings on the book of Luke, I've wondered whether he just purposed to live Jesus' ministry the best he knew how. Perhaps he wanted to bring the mystery of the healing Eucharist to those outside the city gates of the Catholic Church.

Christians aren't supposed to lose faith in Jesus' healing ministry. The loss of faith brings the sense of being an outsider in insider's clothes.

God tried to teach me the mystery of faith since the beginning. He came to abide with the sick, the outsiders. I missed the lesson, though, and compensated by adopting and adding to cessationist yarns, went on believing that my theological constraints of God were somehow ordained. I held so fast to the outsider notions that I refused to enter the communion line in the eighth grade, refused to enter the mystery of God through the Eucharist.

I believed God had stopped visiting demoniacs and Gentiles. If I had taken the time to discuss this with Father Jack, I know he might have told me otherwise. He might have said God is closer to all of us than we realized.

The therapist broke my nostalgic train of thought, the session drawing to an end.

"Throughout the rest of the week, try to break down your systematized thoughts. Have you ever thought God might be at work outside of a particular theology? There might be a little mystery."

"What do you mean?" I asked.

"Sometimes he heals, and sometimes doesn't. Right? And why is this so? Who knows? That hurts, doesn't it?"

"Yes," I said.

"Perhaps sometimes there just aren't answers for life. Sometimes you can't wrap it into a theological bow. Unpack the emotional feelings six to eight levels deep. How do you feel about the mystery, about the pain it's showing you? Empty? Alone? Ashamed? Lost? Dark? Cold? Practice the exercise every day; jot the emotional words that come to mind. Consider where the pain comes from. Does the pain come from the faith healer, or was he just the catalyst for your sense of abandonment? Consider the mystery. There's time for forgiveness work later."

He walked me to the door, shook my hand, and said, "Remember, Jesus abides with those in pain."

I considered the demoniac, Jairus, the bleeding woman. Perhaps he's right; God has been trying to tell me this since the eighth grade.

OCTOBER 30

Considering God's mysteries feels heavy. Why didn't Jesus come and make everything right; why didn't he eradicate all disease? The bleeding woman, Jairus—they had the advantage of asking Jesus for healing face to face. Yet if they had to pray to thin air, to make their petitions to an invisible God, would the outcome have been different? Would the Gospel writers even have recorded any unmet requests?

Why does God heal some and not others? More important, why didn't God heal me? Why is he so slow in healing Titus? These questions are constant embers.

If only I could systematize God, if I could explain with logical certitude why he *does* or *does not*, then I could explain away the hurt, the inequities of the past, the ones of the future. I could create theological constructs whereby God chooses some and not others, whereby he ordains some healings and some deaths, and whereby a lack of faith leads to a lack of healing. I could remove the mystery of spirituality, the complexity of both the God feast and the God famine.

But systems are not God; I know this to be true even though I've spent too much of my life attempting to prove otherwise.

When I was five and playing in the mesquite trees, I heard the clear voice of God, and even then, I had no way of explaining his whisper in the wind moving across the grass, or the way my heart turned grateful at the sight of the scissortail flycatcher daring to dart so close to the ground before returning to the wire. I had no system for explaining the God I saw in all things, or for the love I felt among them. I had no new charismatic language then.

I remember an old Texan woman, a tiny wisp of a twig with switch branches for arms and legs. Her eyes were large and gray. She sat in the country pew in front of us on Sundays, and if we were good during the service, she'd turn and offer us a stick of Wrigley's spearmint gum. She had a genuine smile, and she never spoke a word—at least not as far as I remember. I have no system for explaining how godward her simple charity felt.

When I was a child, I had faith like a child. This charismatic healer—a misguided ninny, really—stripped the tender reed of faith bare. Now I hear only the Spirit-whisper of a mysterious faith, and it's calling me back to mystery.

But how?

<hr>

I know it's time to begin turning in to the pain, headlong, rather than numbing it away. It's time to go back. How? Simple practice. Begin with the last hurt and ask myself, What emotions do I feel? Are the emotions chaotic, disorganized? Are they like a tempestuous sea or a burning atmospheric reentry? Can I sit in those emotions and write them down? I'll consider the emotions, confess them, find the truth in the moment. And then maybe I'll move into the practice of forgiveness. Maybe.

In the forgiveness, I wonder, will I find myself being made more like the Jesus I claim to follow? Is such a thing possible?

NOVEMBER 2

On most mornings, I wake early, brew a pot of coffee, and find my way to the plush blue chair in the corner of the living room. This is the quiet space for listening or sorting things out. Sometimes I hear the wind blowing through the trees outside. On this particular autumn morning, I hear it blowing through the trees, hear the acorns pelting the skylight, they being undone from their branches and sent flying like wooden hail.

The wind rustles the mesquite tree branches of my memory, the essence of my young faith, the place I'm trying to return to. Go into the pain. This is the advice of therapists, sages, and poets. Eleventh-century Persian poet Rumi wrote, "The remedy for the pain is the pain." Starting your morning with a steaming cup of coffee and an accoutrement of pain, however, can be a jolt more than one can bear, so instead, I reach for a distraction: Robert Mulholland's book *Invitation to a Journey*, a book about spiritual formation.

Distractions—aren't they all around? When life slides its shiv into the soft spot between two ribs, when the pain shoots through every nerve, common sense dictates that we run to the doctor or therapist. Common sense dictates that we allow them to take it out and bind our wounds. Why, then, do we so often ignore the shivs? Why do we allow them to bleed us dry while we reach for our manmade salves?

I open to chapter 3 of Mulholland's book, where he writes, "The process of being conformed to the image of Christ takes place primarily at the points of unlikeness to Christ's image. God is present to us in the most destructive aspects of our cultural captivity.

God is involved with us in the most imprisoning bondage of our brokenness. God meets us in those places of our lives most alienated from him. God is there, in grace, offering us the forgiveness, the cleansing, the liberation, the healing we need to begin the journey toward our wholeness and fulfillment in Christ."

This is the challenge, I think: to find the places of unlikeness to God, the places where I am most alienated from him. I am reminded of Paul's words on the matter. In his letter to the Romans, he wrote, "Do not conform to the pattern of this world, but be transformed by the renewing of your mind. Then you will be able to test and approve what God's will is—his good, pleasing and perfect will" (Rom. 12:2).

Transformed—that is the hard work of a phoenix, is it not?

Most mornings, my reading and prayer hour wakes at a slower pace. I begin in the chair, eyes closed and smelling coffee while the remnants of dreams linger. Often my attempts to wipe the groggy fog of sleep clean with prayer feels more like an exercise in effort, in the application of mental elbow grease. Often my prayers turn to nonsensical gibberish about long-lost aunts or churches I never attended or pasta or the like. This morning, though, the fog is being cut, being blown away by a sharper, cleaner wind. The words of Mullholland, the echoes of Paul—they are like smelling salts awakening the unconscious.

In what ways am I most alienated from God?

This question alone is enough to induce anxiety. The skin tingle is an indicator of the pain that is right at the surface. I consider nonconformity and alienation, and everything is ablaze.

In what ways am I alienated from God? I am a Christian who has used systems and liquor—both addictions in their own right—to numb the pain that God might not answer my prayers, that he might not heal, and that ultimately, he might not be present in my life. The pain is evidence of this area of nonconformity, and I have used these vices to dull the pain.

Here, though, in the quiet before the waking of the house, I sense a gentle truth taking hold. God wants to conform me, and that process, as Mulholland wrote, means God is involved in my life. This brings to mind the words of Jesus. "I will never leave you nor forsake you," he said, and this morning, I'm beginning to sense this truth.

Yes, therapist; yes, Rumi; I will go into the pain, but I will not go alone.

In this early hour of risk, I return my questions to God. "Why do I feel the fire of anxiety when I consider Christ, when I consider his working or his not working, his healing or his not healing?" I sit and wait, but the questions only smolder.

Go back to the mesquite trees.

It is the still small voice, carried on a Spirit wind. It is less of a hearing, more of a knowing.

Go back to the mesquite trees of your childlike faith and commune with me.

It occurs to me: Jesus had his own tree grove once.

The Mount of Olives. I turn to the Gospel story. There is Jesus on Passion Eve. He is kneeling, praying, "Father, if you are willing, take this cup from me; yet not my will, but yours be done" (Luke 22:42). Take away the pain, he prays, and when his prayer is not answered, he gives in to the mystery, and an angel comes to give him solace.

I consider my appetite for liquor and realize my overdrinking is not the area of my nonconformity. Instead, it's my inability to accept that God's plan might be opposed to my own human will, my desire for immediate healing. And the mismatch between my will and God's gives rise to the anxiety, to the pain.

I consider Jesus again, how he rescued everyone who asked, but refrained from imposing his own will and rescuing himself. What a mystery! I see him, yielded in the garden on the Mount of Olives. He walked into a death that was not of his choosing, not of his own will. Instead, he walked headlong into death, turned broadside into the Roman spear that was the pointed will of God. And walking through the pain and into the will of God, Jesus showed his healing power both to those who sought to do violence to him, and to innocent bystanders. He healed the dismembered ear of a slave of the high priest (Luke 22:51); he provided for the pardon of the thief Barabbas (Luke 23:25). He asked his father to forgive his murderers (Luke 23:34). He forgave all humankind, from prehistory to eternity (1 Peter 3:18–19). He conformed himself to the will of God and, in it, defeated death and its sting, healed all of creation!

In the comfort of my living room, rich coffee aroma lingering, I hear it again.

Like Jesus, do not avoid the pain. Like Jesus, do not avoid the mystery. Allow conformity to my will. Go and you will find I am with you. I will heal you, and you will bring healing to others.

This kind of going, though, takes yielding to the possibility that God's will might look a lot like a death.

⌒

Do you like childhood games? I do.

Let's play a game somewhat akin to If You Give a Mouse a Cookie. If I give Seth the option, he'll choose the certainty of a particular theology, whether that of the faith healer or the cessationist preacher. If he chooses certainty over the mystery of faith, he'll be let down. If he is let down, he will feel the pain, the fires of nonconformity and incongruity. If he feels the pain of his unfulfilled will, he'll dull the fires with alcohol. If he dulls the fires with alcohol, he'll feel like a Christian fraud. If he feels like a Christian fraud, he'll blame the faith healer and the cessationist preacher, those who taught him only easy theologies of God. If he blames the faith healer and cessationist preacher, he'll fail to forgive them their folly. If he fails to forgive them their folly, he'll find no reconciliation. If there is no reconciliation, the voice of God will remain as quiet as the coming of winter frost. And if this is so, he'll feel the fires of pain and reach for the bottle of gin again.

And so on and so forth. In this death spiral, I have found myself in the great drunk alone.

He is calling me back—back to the essence of faith. And somehow I know the path begins with sitting in the pain of God's mystery. Sometimes our thorns are not removed. Sometimes our children fall ill. Sometimes they die. Sometimes we lose homes, jobs, or churches. Sometimes we turn cancerous or our spouses walk out the door.

I have tried to dissect these ways in which life wounds us, to construct some foolproof theological explanation, and I cannot. There is only mystery left, and if this is so, then being a follower of Christ must mean yielding to the mystery. In this, we are conformed to Christ's garden likeness. And then, in that likeness, we can be agents of forgiveness, agents of reconciliation and healing.

There is a way back to the mesquite trees, to the faith of my youth. It goes into the pain, embraces the mystery without needing theological certainties for each of life's happenings. It requires forgiveness of ghosts and demons. After all, how can I be healed without releasing the agents of pain in my past?

Here is where it all starts: in prayer.

I am resistant to bending into your mystery, God. There is pain there. Heal it. There is fire. Quench it. There is nonconformity. Conform it. Lead me into reconciliation. Lord Jesus Christ, Son of God, have mercy on me, a sinner.

NOVEMBER 6

Forgiveness—it is so abstract a thing in the face of concrete realities. And this is the realm in which, for me, it is tested: the mystery of faith pitted against leukocyte levels, pounds and centimeters, brain tissue, blood vessels.

Titus has been accepted to the Mayo Clinic, and his appointment is next Monday. Amber leaves on Sunday and will carry him northward to Rochester, Minnesota. They'll drive through midwestern cornfields and sleepy towns and into the heart of the Great White North. I've always wanted to see Minnesota, a land I imagine that's filled with ice-fishing huts and fur trappers, but it's not to be this time. I'll be here, tending to Isaac, Jude, and Ian.

In addition to his continuing weight-gain issues and a slight (and likely benign) brain malformation, the neurosurgeons wonder whether his skull is growing properly. At least one doctor believes that instead of growing orbitally, it might be expanding more from front to back, more like the head of an Egyptian pharaoh. Although most would not notice the growth pattern, it might be enough to put pressure on his brain.

This week we also discovered that his leukocytes percentages may be below normal levels, and his vaccinations have not taken hold. Then again, we seem to get conflicting reports from the Arkansas doctors. We hope the doctors at Mayo can put an end to this mystery. In any event, these things, along with his history of infection, have been cause for our referral to the state-of-the-art medical clinic.

For more than a year and a half we've dragged these issues

with Titus behind us like too many chains. They are heavy, and too often we try to hide the clank of their dragging from friends and family, afraid that we'll be seen as the needy ones.

In any event, we are on the eve of another great round of this mess, and we're going right into the heart of it. If there is anyone who deserves healing and wholeness, it is Titus. He is a gem of a boy, a rocket-powered child who runs as much as he walks. His joy is inexhaustible, especially for a boy who's spent so much of his young life hooked to a feeding tube. He is a born joker who's learned the power of sideways glances with his oversized brown eyes. He has already learned to lean into the art of life: the crayon on paper, pen on pad, marker on wall.

There are no easy answers for the lack of his healing, or any other child's, for that matter. I think of Matt—my David House compatriot—whose baby boy Eliot died just ninety-nine days after being born. I consider John and Jane Ray, whose daughter Olivia was taken too soon by a careless driver. I often wonder how those losses could be predestined before the foundation of the world. There are no easy answers for the suffering here, for the famines, the earthquakes, the wars. We can pin it on God's sovereignty, but isn't that a sick way of scapegoating? We can pin it on the evolution of the world under the weight of Eden's sin, but isn't that an embarrassing show of ego? That kind of grandiose onus shouldn't be placed on either God's plan or the free will of man—should it?

Couldn't God come and make it straight? Couldn't he set all things right for the love of himself? It has been two thousand years since Jesus was here, and I don't count on his coming back anytime soon, at least not in my lifetime. The preachers tell me this is folly, but isn't living for the magical return that sets everything straight, that heals my son—isn't that its own form of nihilistic folly or escape-hatch theology? Isn't trusting God through the tragedy and drudgery of life a purer form of faith?

You might build a framework around these questions, attempt

to explain exactly why there is suffering in the world. I certainly have. You might build doctrines to God, up and up and up to the sky like a grand tower. Others might gather around the base and worship the tower, might say they've built a bridge of explanation to the heavens.

I've tried to systematize the pain, and it only brought more pain; systems are great until they cut in unfair ways, see. The answers for God's lack of movement help us make sense of God, until, of course, we *need* him to move. In those moments, if he doesn't act in accordance with our felt need, we see him as absentee, capricious, or a predestining God of sorrow.

Instead, I'm giving in to the great mystery.

My will is that Titus be healed. My will, when I was a child, was for my own healing. What is God's will? I do not know. Yes, I'll still pray without ceasing; I'll muster every bit of faith I can. I'll hope I'm Jairus with the sick child, but if I'm not, I'll give in.

Lord, not my will but yours be done.

Yesterday, my therapist talked to me of David's child, the offspring of his illicit night with Bathsheba. He said, "This is my go-to story of healing prayer in the Bible."

I stole time later in the day and read. David's child was stricken with a morbid sickness. David, doting father as he was, retreated to his chambers, wailed and wept for healing. He tore his clothes, engaged in mourning. Word came to his servants that the child had died, and they whispered among themselves.

"How will we tell David about the death of his son? He'll surely kill himself!"

David noticed their secret sharing, said, "He has died, hasn't he?"

The servants confirmed it, and David ceased his wailing. He rose, put on fresh clothes, and called for a meal. The servants asked why David mourned as if he intended to go about his life as usual after the child's death. David said, "I prayed because I thought God might change his mind, but he didn't. Why should I weep now? I'll see him again one day."

David struggled in prayer for his son, but in the end, he gave in to the mystery that God did not relent. David embraced the present reality of death, while looking forward to the future reality of wholeness. Isn't this embracing the mystery? Isn't this the way of conformity to the will of God?

Perhaps my story and David's are similar. Perhaps not. But whether or not Titus is made whole in this life, embracing the mystery means embracing both present death and eternal life.

———

How did I come to be trained to hold so fast to my will despite all of nature's efforts to train me otherwise? The wind blows where it wills, holds the kite up, sends it ducking and dodging. The Spirit blows much the same too.

I once stood in our front yard, the Texas hardpan pocked with fire ant hills. It was summer, and my sister and I had been chasing each other in the yard. She was bigger, stronger, and faster, and I was unable to catch her unless she allowed me to. She skirted my reach time after time, yelling, "Nah-nah-ne-boo-boo; you can't catch me!" And then when my frustration of being too small and too slow had reached the point of near hatred, she began taunting me while standing within spitting distance of a fire ant hill. I walked toward her, telling her I gave up, but at the last second, I gave the ant hill a good kick in her direction. But the wind wasn't on my side. Just as I kicked the ant hill, the wind kicked itself up with a great gust, driving hundreds of tiny, angry jowls back onto my legs.

How futile is the will when pitted against the unpredictable mystery of God's creation. It is a lesson I am still learning.

The will is too small a thing to go up against nature. My grandmother was done in by the cancer. It metastasized in her lungs and moved to every part of her body. It was the smoking that had given the cancer a foothold, I think. It was the mystery that drove it throughout her body, ending her life before she or I or anyone else otherwise willed it. This is the way nature works, the way of mystery. Even kings submit to it.

"If they can't figure it out at Mayo," Amber says, "it can't be figured." She says this as she loads Titus into the minivan for the drive to Minnesota. She leans in, hugs me long, and buries her head in my sweater. "I love you," she says. "Pray and be good." I tell her I will, and not to worry about me.

"I won't drink."

"I know," she says, then reaches upward and kisses me on the lips before slipping into the driver's seat. She pulls from the drive, and I watch her taillights turn left as she leaves the neighborhood.

I have taken to praying for Titus more and more. As Amber pulls from the neighborhood, I begin praying my guts out. I can think of no better way to put it. This is no small thing. I am praying that Titus will be healed, even though I still hear the faith healer taunting my faith, still see the lesser version of me wasting away under his accusations.

"If you had enough faith, your son might be healed," I hear. The implications rise: I am not a man of strong faith.

I wonder whether the folks who blame everything on faith or the lack thereof are doing the best they know how. Sometimes I wonder whether their good intentions have gone awry and mucked up this whole religion thing for the rest of us. If they thought it through, would they continue to foist the pressure of having mountain-moving faith on others?

I hear the echoes in the cavernous spaces of my heart and I sit with them. I listen to the accusations: that my faith is too small, that God is a liar, that he might not be God at all. I sit with them, allow them to say their piece, listen as they try to tempt my will to throw a temper tantrum, to kick against God's shins.

I close my eyes and listen.

I will never leave you nor forsake you.

I hear it. I sit in it.

Go back to the mesquite trees.

I hear this too, and I imagine myself in the grove, braiding strands of long grass into a rope which I will attach to my Han Solo action figure so that he can rappel down the knotty side of one of the trees. I hear the wind, how it whispers through the grass and tells me I am not alone. I hear myself singing the songs of my youth while my hands are at work: *humble yourself in the sight of the Lord, and he will lift you up.* I always loved that song.

In those days, I was with God, and despite the world's best attempts to either upend faith or saddle me with the pressure of mustering enough faith to prove my fidelity to God, I know the truth. God is still with me now.

The voices in the darker spaces grow higher pitched, but fainter. They are desperate liars, and I can hear the voices thinning. I sit in prayer, repeat the words of Christ at Gethsemane: *not my will but yours.* I pray it, and then sink into the mystery of knowing God, of God knowing me.

In the days of early faith, my proofs of God were in the wind, the simple songs, the whispers that the "ears of my ears" were born to hear. My proofs were the generosity of the church ladies, the midnight prayers of my parents over my dreams, the way the thunder rolled across the Texas plain, making me feel so small. The open sky, Kool-Aid at vacation Bible school—the nearness of God was palpable in these. God was close in the days when it was okay to rest in my smallness, when I needed no theological answer for every trauma of life. God was close when my will was, by its nature, bent low before an immeasurable mystery.

Yes, I will bow low like a child, bend my will to the will of God. And in the surrender—*Lord, not my will*—in the meeting of

God, whether in Gethsemane or Eden, I'll pray with more abandon. Perhaps I'll rejoice in knowing the measure of *Emmanuel, God with us* in darker days. Perhaps I'll see light breaking through the cave mouth, coming broader and brighter like the rising of some inner sun. Perhaps I'll see that the God who was then and is now and is to come, whether in life or death, in sickness or healing, is here.

Yes, his promise is that he has never left me nor forsaken me. The thought steels my legs, props me upright. The thought brings me into the beauty that is God's presence, and the words of E. E. Cummings' great poem come before I can turn my thoughts back toward Scripture or prayer or any other sanctioned spiritual discipline.

> *i thank You God for most this amazing*
>
> *day: for the leaping greenly spirits of trees*
> *and a blue true dream of sky; and for everything*
> *which is natural which is infinite which is yes*
>
> *(i who have died am alive again today,*
> *and this is the sun's birthday; this is the birth*
> *day of life and of love and wings: and of the gay*
> *great happening illimitably earth)*
>
> *how should tasting touching hearing seeing*
> *breathing any—lifted from the no*
> *of all nothing—human merely being*
> *doubt unimaginable You?*
>
> *(now the ears of my ears awake and*
> *now the eyes of my eyes are opened)*

Yes. This is the way I'll pray, today.

Lord Jesus Christ, Son of God, have mercy on me, a sinner. Open the eyes of my eyes to the unimaginable you, who is always and forever, who never leaves nor forsakes. Let me not doubt unimaginable you.

NOVEMBER 13

It's my fourteenth wedding anniversary, and Amber and I are hundreds of miles apart. I am in the Ozark autumn, sitting in the back yard under the browning broad leaves of a massive American sycamore, watching as Isaac, Jude, and Ian play tag. Amber is with Titus in Minnesota. This is not the romantic anniversary celebration I would have imagined at the beginning of this year.

At the Mayo Clinic, Amber and Titus meet with various doctors—endocrinologists, neurologists, immunologists, and geneticists. They are looking for the unnamed malady at the root of Titus's failure to thrive, a phrase we're hearing a lot these days.

Failure to thrive is loaded with meaning. Failure is such a defeating word. Even at this young age, Titus is saddled with it; he cannot conjure success at the simplest thing for most Americans: fattening up. The sweet ladies at church are forever telling us to send him home with them. They will feed him boiled meat and fried pies and whole milk, they say. We've tried these things, we tell them, and they laugh and respond, "But he's never had *my* pies."

It's annoying.

Titus has confounded us, the sweet church ladies, a local medical staff, and a regional medical staff. Today is a hopeful day, though. Today, Titus and Amber are in the land of what Amber calls the Nor-people (she calls them this on account of their distinct Norwegian features: blond hair, square shoulders, and polite manners), people with a knack for making a go of it in harsh conditions. It's fitting that they've grown a state-of-the-art medical facility there, one that specializes in solving the most difficult conditions. We're hopeful that we'll finally get some answers.

Amber calls, says that this morning a neurologist spent almost an hour with Titus before declaring him to be well-adjusted and cognitively sound. The doctor reckoned that perhaps his brain malformation isn't quite as bad as the good folks in Arkansas might think, and in any event, it is improbable that it has any effect on his ability to thrive. Perhaps the geneticist, immunologist, or gastroenterologist will come up with some better answer, Amber says. This seems to be the way of our world. Visit the doctor only to be told that, yes, there is a problem, but no, there aren't any clear solutions.

I can hear the exhaustion in Amber's voice. She and Titus are out of their element, trapped in a series of sterile rooms and labs all connected by underground tunnels so that one isn't required to brave the negative temperatures of a Minnesota winter. Titus is itching to play, as any two-year-old would, and all these rooms and tunnels have made him cagier. Amber says Titus is a ball of energy—maybe too much. He is like a mouse in a maze, or a ping-pong ball bouncing from wall to wall, Amber says.

Titus is the smallest ball of joy. He is a vivacious child. If he were not, this process would be even more maddening.

Last night I sat alone in my bed, upright and drawing the shades on the day with a bit of Scripture and prayer. I read Paul's letter to the Romans: "For the creation was subjected to frustration, not by its own choice, but by the will of the one who subjected it, in hope that the creation itself will be liberated from its bondage to decay and brought into the freedom and glory of the children of God. We know that the whole creation has been groaning as in the pains of childbirth right up to the present time. Not only so, but we ourselves, who have the firstfruits of the Spirit, groan inwardly as we wait eagerly for our adoption to sonship, the redemption of our bodies" (Rom. 8:20–23).

The stomach of the world churns. We all live in the maddening groan. If we sit in the silence long enough, if we listen, we hear it. The patina of the Ozark summer before the leaves brown and fall, the thick snow blanket of the dead Minnesota winter, the quaking of the fault lines—these are all the sounds of groaning for redemption.

We also, brothers and sisters to all creation, groan. The failing health of an Arkansas toddler, the slipping mind of the aging parent with dementia, the gray hairs that come in the dealing with toddlers and parents alike—these are sure signs that every cell within us groans.

Jesus groaned in the garden too. Isn't it ironic? The Great Reconciler himself asking to forego the very act that would bring reconciliation? He wanting redemption by some other purchase? How do we handle that? He too was fully human.

The mystery deepens and deepens.

I consider Jesus in Gethsemane. *Lord, if it be your will, let this cup pass.* It is the most human prayer of Jesus, I think. It is the bend-low before God, the stinging sweat prayer where Jesus says, "If you could spare me a favor, I'd rather not endure this." I consider his prayer of self-preservation; if his request had been granted, what of this groaning creation? Would we still have been united with God, rescued from the slavery and corruption of the world? Or would we have groaned and groaned and groaned into and throughout eternity?

In his humanity, though, Jesus learned to bend his will to God's so that he could be the ultimate agent of reconciliation. He surrendered to the mystery of God's will, that he would be crucified, murdered, and that his murder would somehow bring a better way.

To ask for relief from God—this is human. To pray through the pain, to live in it instead of numbing yourself to it, to subjugate your will to the will of God, even in the face of potential suffering—this is what it means to be like Jesus. This is what it means to yield to the mystery.

I consider Titus again and feel the acute point of pain, hear the groaning rising in my guts. I quiet my questions, still my mind, and let a simple petition fly: *Lord Jesus Christ, Son of God, heal my son. We are all groaning for the redemption of Titus's body in the here and now. Cure him like you did the woman of faith and Jairus's daughter.*

I pause and listen, and hearing nothing, I pray again.

Lord Jesus Christ, Son of God, heal my son.

"No," comes the voice, "at least not like you think." The Spirit in this moment is less like a small whisper and more like a jarring foghorn.

That's it. There is no more nuance to the statement, no additional explanation. It is a simple denial, almost terse, and this is the moment I best understand my Catholic friends' notion of purgatory. I am high-centered on the tension wire between death and resurrection.

It bears admitting—this word from God could be nothing more than the tired mind playing tricks. I have not slept well these past few nights without Amber, and the stress of being away from Titus while he's being treated nags. In moments like these, psychologists and friends alike remind us that our noggins can be deceptive, give us mirages of answers instead of answers themselves. This is why our more conservative, systematic brothers in faith tell us not to trust listening prayers. There is a danger that one might conflate the voice of God with your own, they say, and I am not naïve to this. This, some believe, is the reason we listen for answers only and always through the Scriptures, never through the still small voices that speak to us in the night. I find this notion ironic. No one *ever* has misread, misheard, and misapplied a passage of Scripture and claimed it as an answer to the burning questions of the day, right? But these systems, the rigid understandings of prayer and meditation only ever led me to a great internal conflict, to denying my earliest childlike faith, which knew a more intimate creator.

Yes, the systematizers warn us, "Do not trust the voices in your head." You've heard this too. But what if the answers in your head are the voice of God himself? What if they square with circumstance and Scripture, or do not contradict them? What if they are confirmed by your community and all the world around you?

I sat upright in my bed and prayed with expectation. I waited for an answer, begged for one, really. All I heard was a stark answer. It was not the word I had hoped to hear. Truth be told, I'm not sure I hoped to hear anything. Nonetheless, it was a word, forceful but true.

I have been dry for fifty-three days, and fifty-four days ago, approaching God to ask for healing would have spun me by the spoke until I fell headlong into the bottle. Fifty-four days ago, I would have drowned the question and its potential pain in a highball with gin and rocks. But today even this most feared word in answer does not bring fire to my skin.

This, I think, is a little victory.

The prayer, the response, the little victory—perhaps there is another healing at stake here. Perhaps this is the sensation of incremental transformation, or at least its small start.

I am groaning to be made whole too; I know it. Just like Titus and Amber and the broken earth on which we stand. In the dry-sober, I'm learning to listen to this groaning, to sit in it with the great reconciler of it. In the sitting, I'm finding a good word: *if I tell you no, but I'm here with you, isn't that enough? Blessed are those who do not see and still believe. Blessed are you. Today the answer may be no, but in me, all things are forever summed up as yes.*

Here I am, in an awkward kind of coming clean. I am watching demons flee into drunk pigs. I will take one thousand divine denials. I'll live in the groaning. If it means I get to hear God's clear voice, I'll subject my will to the mystery of his. I believe that his voice, even in the no, is better than silence.

Lord Jesus Christ, Son of God, have mercy on me, a sinner. Drive out the Gerasenian demons, bend my will around yours, teach me to count your voice as the ultimate gift.

A week later his disciples were in the house again, and Thomas was with them. . . . Jesus came and stood among them and said, "Peace be with you!" Then he said to Thomas, "Put your finger here; see my hands. Reach out your hand and put it into my side. Stop doubting and believe." Thomas said to him, "My Lord and my God!" Then Jesus told him, "Because you have seen me, you have believed; blessed are those who have not seen and yet have believed."

—JOHN 20:26–29

It is easier, somehow, to accept a no from a God who makes all things new. Isn't it he who wants healing and wholeness, who reconciles all things? If all things are summed up in God as yes, then what happens at the intersection of no and prayer? Does the penitent pray-er of prayers stop petitioning? Is the Almighty's denial meant to undercut the faith of the weak-kneed?

It is evening, and I can hear Ian snoring in his bed. I hear the creak of the bunk beds and know that Jude and Isaac are tossing and turning themselves to dreams. They are such precious children, and I consider how one day, they'll experience their own denials of prayer.

Lord, protect them from cynicism and anxiety in this; teach them to be persistent.

Taking my own advice, I avoid the *no,* push through and

continue my requests for Titus's healing. Perhaps this makes me an obstinate fool, a kicker against the goads. But I suppose this also puts me in good company.

When the Israelites scorned Moses by worshiping a metallic calf, God, in his fury, purposed to kill them all, to replace Abraham's line with that of Moses. Did Moses not petition God to change his mind? Maybe Moses was obstinate, but did God not consider Moses' plea? Did he not relent (Exodus 32)? Yes, Moses was obstinate, but the Exodus account records that, even still, God spoke to Moses "face to face, just as a man speaks to his friend" (Exod. 33:11 NASB).

Audacious enough to speak face to face, I pray again. "God, please heal my son." Praying these things on the heels of divine denial raises the question of effectiveness (not to mention immaturity or stupidity).

Amber called earlier and said the doctors at Mayo have noted some genetic anomalies, and one has postulated a rare syndrome that, though complicating, is not always life-threatening. She delivered this as good news, and the fact that Titus does not suffer from a disease that will end his life in the near future is a blessing. That being said, the doctors believe he might have an esophageal abnormality that will need continuing care and consistent monitoring.

I consider this, and there is some relief. Considering the clouds instead of the silver lining, though, I think about Titus's DNA coding. Is there a flaw that keeps him from taking in all the nutrients he needs? Perhaps God, though able, is not willing to unwind the genetic code, to straighten the double helix gone astray. Does God undo what genes have already done?

I question whether there is a single purported case of miraculous healing of a genetic mutation. Are there some things God purposes to remain unchanged forever? Are there things to which his eternal answer is, "Let's let it ride?" The Christ of Scripture was a master of casting things out—demons and sin in particular—and restoring life to the dead. He healed maladies—blindness, deafness, and leprosy. Did he ever cure a genetic defect? Would he? If God created all beings, all things for his glory, then aren't those with genetic maladies somehow a display of his glory?

The questions flood and my evening prayers are drowning. I feel the rising anxiety. It is only one night after great peace in the face of a denied prayer, and I feel the need for liquor. This is not a loose and gentle craving but the burning ache of compulsion. It is my body's tell: there is pain coming and I need to sit in it.

The pain is this: what if God can't, or simply will not, heal? The grass withers and the flower fades, and what if Titus withers too? What if the word of God's *no* stands forever?

It seems this life of faith is ever held in a great tug-of-war tension. Yesterday, I was in victorious communion with the mystery of God's will. Today, I am flailing. The human condition is such an enigma.

Hopelessness creeps in with its company of thieves: disillusionment, anger, and deception. And these things all arose from a simple, perhaps willful prayer—*God heal my son?*

This is why I gave up prayer's ghost last year. I know that now.

I remember the words I heard in therapy: *when anxiety rises, when things spin ever out of control, go back to the mesquite trees of your childlike faith.* I recall them, the early days of faith. I can almost smell the dust-heavy wind, almost hear the cattle calling from the other side of the great mud hole. I can hear the call of God in the winds blowing through the trees. He was with me then, and I remember his promise: *I will never leave you nor forsake you.*

I feel the fires dulling, the cravings being put to death. God is here.

I have found that even in the obstinate prayer, even in the prayer that is not answered to my liking, I can survive the pain without the liquor; I can allow my will to be bent to his so long as

I know that God abides even in the mystery of the divine no. He is here, even in this.

Does bending the will of man to the will of God mean that praying for the desired outcome ceases? Quite the contrary. If those prayers ceased, men would never be required to face their inability to change the eternal aspects of life. If those prayers ceased, how would men pray in the hope that, yes, sometimes God changes his mind? If those prayers ceased, would we understand the abiding presence of God as being with us in conversation, or would we rather see him as the dictator of divine edicts? The Good Book shows us example after example of God-fearing men who prayed in the face of certain answers. Sometimes God changes his mind or relents. Sometimes he does not.

All this is part of the mystery. Who can understand it?

Consider Moses. God heard his prayer and relented, sparing the nation of Israel.

Consider David as he prayed for God to spare the child carried by Bathsheba. Did he hear his prayer?

Consider Jesus in the garden. Jesus, the Son of God himself, prayed and received the divine no.

Titus's healing would bring steel to the legs of my faith. But in praying through the divine no, in asking God to relent, I am finding that my will is becoming more malleable; I am becoming more open to the *not my will but yours be done*. This is the slower process of shoring up genuine faith, and it seems a different expression of faith than that of the faith healers of long ago.

This is an expression of faith that hurts.

The bones of faith are brittle. This is a product of the human condition. When our prayers go unanswered, when God does not meet us at the point of our desires, we turn to the lowercase gods to ease the pain of living. Bow to the god of booze; bow to the god of sex; bow to your food, to your material possessions! I traded my prayers for a liquid fire-god, because the idea of having my will bent around God's (as if I'd yet discerned it) was unbearable.

But here, I'm asking the Lord to reconsider the divine no. I'm asking for healing again. And in these prayers, I am reminded that prayer is less of a signpost of radical faith and more of a measure of communion with God. In these prayers for healing, I confess how I have felt toward the divine will, and God visits, bends my will by his abiding presence.

I feel once manipulated by the platitudes of a faith healer, and I tell God.

I feel the anger of faith unanswered, and I tell God.

Yet I feel relief that God is present, that he is speaking even in the divine no, and I tell him that too.

Go back to the mesquite trees, I hear again.

I remember this God of the mesquite groves, how he played with me in a world that I didn't know needed reconciling or forgiving. I consider his presence then, his presence now, and am hopeful that the bending of my will to his is yet another sign that he is with me, even to the end of the age.

"I will never leave you nor forsake you," he says, "in sickness or in health."

The invitation to make our will known to God, to beg for his intervention, is an invitation to act like the blood-sweating Jesus in the garden. Bending the will, though, requires the Christlike willingness to endure the cup of unmet expectations. Bending the will requires a Christlike faith, a faith that says, "Father knows best." Bending requires Chirstlike knowledge that even in the shadow of every valley, God works all things together for good (Rom. 8:28).

I will continue to pray for my son because this is where I most meet God. This is a crucible of sorts, a place where the fire of unmet expectations is always stoked. But this fire is the place where my will becomes more malleable. There will always be the temptation to give in to the weaker parts of the flesh, to numb it all with a drink, but I know, now, that God will abide, even if I fall off the wagon of sobriety or belief.

God is in the valley of the shadow, yes. I believe he's in the joy in the morning too. How do I know? I'm not one to second-guess his promises.

"I will never leave you nor forsake you," he says and says and says.

NOVEMBER 18

Visits to the therapist have become a thing I rather look forward to. In those initial visits, walking through the doors was an awkward, off-putting experience, in part because I'd never considered myself broken enough to need any sort of psychological evaluation, and in part because I was concerned with what people might think of my visiting a shrink. In the end, though, I reckoned my cognitive engines weren't firing on all cylinders, and I needed to visit a people mechanic. That's all a good therapist is, after all: one who helps you clean out the engine junk, gets you back to smooth running. And the more I sit with him in the weight of my questions, in the confusion of my cognitive dissonance, the more I've come to appreciate these visits.

Today, he asked me how I felt, and I told him I've been struggling less with the bottle these days, that I've been learning to sit in the pain and wait for the truth. I've been learning to bend my will around the truth.

"What is the truth?" he asked.

"God has been with me since the beginning, and he's never gone anywhere. The faith healer didn't take away his presence. The more rigid churchfolk didn't take away his presence. God is with me even when my prayers for healing go unanswered."

"So let's talk about the church."

I didn't want to.

"Tell me the truth about the church, about both the faith healer and the formulaic, systematized religious structure. Did the church do you wrong?"

I considered the question and tossed a quick prayer heavenward: *Lord, let me see.*

He did.

———

Ann Curtis was a trim woman who stood somewhere near five seven, if you included her silver beehive hairdo. It was well known that she took the morning shift at the prayer room. It was even rumored that Mrs. Curtis took two morning shifts and often covered the third on account of the frequent absence of a traveling salesman whose morning calls and morning prayers were often at odds.

She lived across the street from the First Baptist Church, which was convenient because she spent the majority of her day there. Her husband had passed some years before, and instead of becoming some kind of assisted-living hermitess, she reckoned to spend her days serving the church in prayer.

Every morning, Mrs. Curtis walked to the church, stopping sometimes by the bakery to grab a loaf of bread, a pastry, or a pint of milk. She did a great deal of walking, I remember, and I think this was because she had some sort of difficulty driving. Perhaps this was not the sort of difficulty brought on by old age or senility but was the result of having a hairdo that was intolerant of being mashed against the interior roof of her old Buick. So Mrs. Curtis walked just about everywhere, lips moving all the while in prayer.

When I was fifteen, our church youth group held a True Love Waits conference, wherein the lot of us gathered at the church house for the weekend and signed pledge cards vowing we'd wait till marriage to taste the sweet fruits of monogamous marital bliss. Come to find out, those vows were flexible for most of us, but some lasting good came of the event. The conference culminated in the Sunday evening church meeting, and after the pastor explained the event to the church, he invited each of us to the front, where we laid our True Love Waits pledge cards on the stage. The pastor then invited the congregants to make their own pledges.

"Come to the front and take a card," he said. "Pledge to pray for the purity of whatever name you draw until said name is faithfully joined in marriage."

As fate, fortune, and the Holy Ghost would have it, Mrs. Curtis drew my name. She never told me she had drawn my pledge card. She never broached the subject of purity or lust with me, which is good because the awkwardness quotient of any such conversation would have been rivaled only by the time Sister Sarto had the sex talk with my class of sixth grade boys in Catholic school. In any event, Mrs. Curtis never spoke a word to me other than, "Hello, son," or, "Would you hold the door, please?" Sometimes she'd use my arm as a sort of extended handrail for climbing up the church stoop on Sunday morning, and she'd smile her thanks. This was the extent of our real-world interactions. Mrs. Curtis's interactions were never limited to the real world, though.

Seven years and two children into my marriage, I received word that Mrs. Curtis had passed away. In the moment, I regretted that we'd never had a serious conversation. The minister who called to pass along the word of Mrs. Curtis's death had some news. "I want you to know," he said, "that Mrs. Curtis kept your pledge card in her Bible till the day she died. I happen to know that she never missed a day of praying for you, even after you were married."

Ann Curtis was a saint of a woman. A woman who prayed that the abiding presence of God would protect me. It's true: the broader church did nothing to damage my faith. The church is made of some pretty good folks.

Today, the therapist brought me back to center. "Now, about the faith healer—did he set out to harm you?"

"No," I said, "he was just one man wielding haphazard theology, trying to prove a point or line his pockets, or maybe a little of both."

"And what about those folks who've said ridiculous things about faith and healing and Titus's illness being for God's glory? Did they mean to jab you?"

I saw his point, and I let his question hang.

"Here's a better one. What about the folks who say, 'God will never give you more than you can bear'?" He stopped with a wry smile and chuckled. "Aside from the fact that the Bible only uses that verse in relation to temptation, it's just an emotionally stupid thing to say to the sufferer," he said. "Anyhow, folks do their best to help. They're not sure what to say, which, as an aside, does not excuse their behavior, but that doesn't make them bad people."

He paused for some sort of dramatic effect. It was not lost on me.

"So you're back on speaking terms with God. This is good. But what about other people? Now the task is to make your peace with them. You've reconciled with God, but now you need to reconcile with the people who have hurt you the most. You have to forgive them. This is what Jesus did *after* the garden."

"I've tried," I said, which is a sort of technical truth, though my heart has never really been in it. There are ways you can say "I forgive" without allowing the words to take root.

"Try some more," he said with a chuckle. "When you were a child, there was no hurt that kept you from communion with God. That is, until there was. You've held fast to fear of and bitterness toward the faith healer. In fact, you've kept him locked up in your interior spaces, the cave of your soul, and you've allowed him to continue to speak doubt into your life. You haven't given him the freedom to leave. And so you haven't given freedom to *yourself*. You haven't forgiven him—not really. And unforgiveness—this is a sort of barrier to communion with God."

I knew he was right because the thought of engaging in

forgiveness made my stomach turn and triggered the firing of my amygdala. *Fight or flee! Fight or flee!*

Tonight, as I contemplate the therapy session, I feel the burn of the adrenalin, the creak of the cortisol. Going into the cave of the soul, sitting in the pain until I hear from God, allowing my will to be bent to his—this is one thing. Speaking forgiveness over those who were the source of pain in my life? This is a different thing altogether.

I consider the good people of the church, how most of them have never said a mumbling word that would derail my faith. There are good, hard-loving people like Ann Curtis who want only for faith to be protected. I am in *one body* with them, Jesus says, and Paul tells me that I might be the eye to their leg. If that's so, I reckon I owe it to them to be the healthiest eye I can be. Wouldn't it be a grand thing, then, to have my cataracts removed? Wouldn't it be a grand thing to see through a less dense and dim fog?

I know the poison of unforgiveness is still in my system. I can still feel the sting of inept words, and I know it is the thing that could threaten to undo all that has been done. This week, I'll wade into forgiveness in an effort to expel the poison. I suppose it'll bring that uneasy feeling that begs for the bottle. But in the end, I know this is the next step down the road of recovery. I can feel it.

Lord Jesus Christ, Son of God, have mercy on me, a sinner. Teach me to forgive my debtors as you forgive my debts.

PART 3
THE HEALING

Well, from the paradigm that Jesus provided, as he was being crucified, he said, "Father, forgive them." It wasn't as if he was talking about something that might happen. He was actually experiencing one of the most excruciating ways of being killed, and yet he had the capacity to live out a prayer that he taught Christians, that we can expect to be forgiven only insofar as we are ready to forgive.

—DESMOND TUTU

In the mesquite groves, what is there to forgive?

In the early days of faith, I remember no significant pains. I was not beaten or abused, nor was I the product of an abusive relationship. (My mother once told me I was the product of a lavish winter party, but that is a story for another day.) I was raised in simple faith, with simple folks, and the eyes of my memory were opened to the heart of dusty Texas country.

It is true, my father was either absent or asleep a great deal in my younger days. He was a dockworker on the night shift in Dallas. I remember no bitterness or anger over this fact. Even at that age, I knew that a man has to do what a man has to do. I do not remember things as tumultuous or violent or otherwise sour like so many others might. Instead, life was fresh, new, and if I try, I can still smell the greenness of faith in my memory.

I am there, in the field, at odds with no one so long as I stay a healthy distance away from the cattle pond when I'm dressed in my Sunday best. I am on the low branches of the trees and humming nothing in particular, as six-year-olds are prone to do. I talk to God as if he is my playmate, and in a way he is. I ask him about Adam and Eve, ask him if he ever gets hacked off at their first sin, at how they ruined everything. I muster a childlike sense of justice. I know now that God must have smiled at my naïveté.

This, I think, is the hallmark of childhood faith. Untouched by pain, by death, we see with the simplest eyes, take things at face value. We are most alive.

Along the way, though, the poison of seeing, touching, tasting, and experiencing the taint of all knowing—the taint of sin—sets in. There are none unaffected by the sting of sickness, death, and sin. What's more, there are none who do not afflict others with the poison of their own sin. This has been the way of humanity since the garden of Eden.

I felt the first sting when I was told I could be healed and wasn't. I felt the sting when well-intentioned friends said that Titus would be healed because I was a man of faith, and that God had ordained his sickness to bring him more glory, and that God hadn't given me more than I could bear.

There is a universal truth in the human experience: we are all the walking bitten; we are all stung by our fellow humans. And here's the rub: I've stung others along the way, maybe some of you.

Consider it: haven't you felt the poison of the lying, cheating, abusing world? Haven't those with well-meaning words wounded you? Hasn't the venom of manipulation coagulated in your veins? Haven't you harbored bitterness, unforgiveness, doubt in your fellow man, doubt in God? Hasn't it become your best pet malady?

It is mine.

I consider the faith healer, the hospital visitor, the hapless word-wielders. Insensitive brutes they may have been, but aren't they also infected? Aren't they manipulated too? Aren't they, for the most part, just doing the best they know how, even if operating from a low emotional intelligence?

Just ask Cain and Abel: humans hurt humans. Sometimes it is volitional; sometimes it is carried out with genocidal intent or for ill-gotten gain or as a power play. More often, though, I wonder whether we're all grasping at straws, and whether sometimes, in the middle of the desperate, floundering attempts to grab the longest one, we overreach and sucker punch another in the jaw.

Not every pain is the result of ill intent. There are fewer sociopaths and more broken, confused, flailing folks than any of us would like to admit.

NOVEMBER 22

Titus has been at the Mayo Clinic for almost two weeks. The doctors have determined only that his esophagus is being rubbed raw, and this could be the cause of his failure to thrive. They confirm he suffers from a condition known as eosinophilic esophagitis, an inflammatory disease of the esophagus, which can lead to difficulty and pain in swallowing. Its cause is unknown, though it is often associated with a food allergy or acid reflux. He has been given certain dietary restrictions, and if the restrictions do not work, we'll begin more aggressive treatment with medicine.

Perhaps this is the answer, or part of the answer. I have prayed that God would give my son relief, would grant him a miracle growth spurt. So far, that has not been in the cards. Titus has lost another pound since the drive to Mayo. He is slipping into a backward cycle.

Titus has not been healed.

"If you just have faith," the faith healer said. "It's all for God's glory," the well-meaning hospital visitors said. Faith, they tell me, is the silver bullet. After all, did any other faith carrier in the Gospels ask Jesus for healing and not receive it? The cave in my heart is filled with these pious promises echoing off every wall.

I can feel the anger rising at those who would use Scripture to indict those of us who struggle with faith, who crane our necks to hear the slightest whisper of God on the wind.

"Only believe," they say, "and God will work all things together for good."

"What is good?" I've wanted to ask so many times. Instead, I've just nodded and smiled and spat one thousand silent curses.

But sweet Jesus, Mary, and Joseph, I want to believe. Lord, help my unbelief.

The words of others can be such a scourge, and their byproducts—anger, bitterness, unforgiveness—are a poison, aren't they? Can you feel them? Even now, I feel the poison gurgling up like a rancid spring. This poison spring—it is the neurotoxin able to kill the nerves of the spirit.

Let's consider the poison. Shall we?

The Ozark land is home to only two kinds of poisonous spiders—the brown recluse, and the black widow. The black widow—she is Amber's least favorite of all of God's creation.

At the old rock homestead, the house that was in the family for at least four generations, the recycling bin sits against the limestone outer wall. The bin's deep lip serves both as a fastening joint and a handle for carrying it to the curb at Monday's first light. The lip is deep enough to swallow four fingers up to the second knuckle; it is a functional design for humans and black widows alike.

The black widow is a member of a spider family containing thirty-two varieties, and her bite thrusts a sickening neurotoxin under skin. Her pinprick brings nausea, cold sweats, and sometimes difficulty breathing. She weaves a thick, low web, which lacks the sophisticated artistry of her cousin the black and yellow argiope. The black widow is a pragmatic dame, little adorned except for the red hourglass that serves as portent only to the one who might dare flip her on her back. She is a functional home builder who hides in any good nook or cranny. Her sting is light, and some of her victims report never having felt her bite.

Black widow—she rather enjoys lying in wait in the deep lip around the edges of the recycling bin. She waits for unsuspecting insects, for fingers. She is an undetectable shadow-hider, a sister of stealth.

Black widow—she is a ghost. I flip the lid from the bin with the tip of my shoe and toss in old milk cartons, a juice bottle, and a flattened Rice Krispies box. I scan the underside of the lip, look for her hazy home. She is suspended in the silk cloud, her delicate spindle legs raised above her plumpish round rear. She is pounce ready. I root her out with a stick, mash her on the concrete with the sole of my shoe, and smear her across the pavement for good measure. This demolition of the widow's home will last only a few weeks. Then her progeny return to take up residence. They are her specters, projects of hers that seem to return in the night.

Sometimes we run from poison, smash it against the concrete. Other times poisons are not so evident; sometimes they are appealing.

An Ozark spring is an unforgettable thing. God wrinkled the covers of places like Spavinaw Creek, left peaks and valleys covered thick with the brilliance of his third creative day. Most things come in pastel greens in the Ozark spring—the tender leaf buds of the oak and the maple—but some things come in crisper shades of dogwood white and redbud purple. There is God-spoken food in the Ozark spring—wild carrot and potato, dandelions, walnuts. My favorite, though, is the morel, that honeycomb-capped mushroom that soaks up butter better than it suffers direct sunlight. It is a delicacy in these parts, one for which good people pay a blue-collar fortune.

The false morel, though, is a red-capped temptress. Its bosom is a rich burnt red, an inviting hue. The morel bears a distinctive and delicate inward-pitted look like that of a honeycomb. The false morel is cruder, appearing as a discarded sienna paper wad fixed to the top of a short used candle.

The false morel carries a volatile carcinogenic toxin, a slow acting poison that, when ingested, attacks both the bowels and the brain. The toxin induces a well-founded need for Pepto-Bismol, Gatorade, and a quick trip to your doctor. (And yes, this is why your mother warned you against eating wild mushrooms.)

I saw the devil fungus along a local bike trail this spring. I tipped my cap to hers (every beautiful thing deserves its due, even if only from a distance) and carried on. I knew better than to sauté her in butter, as inviting as she might appear. There is no dish made better by the addition of buttered poison.

From an early age, my mother warned me of the sting of the black widow and the poison of the bitter wild mushrooms. Didn't yours? But what of the toxins that are less conspicuous? What of those poisons that are endemic to the human condition, that affect the spiritual nervous system? What of the contagions that kill, steal, and destroy?

Consider the poisons of the human condition. Consider your poison of choice.

Lord Jesus Christ, Son of God, have mercy on me, a sinner. Teach me how to extract the poison; teach me how to come clean.

NOVEMBER 24

There is nothing new under the sun, Solomon said. Neither the seeds nor the fruit of my story are so different from yours. Am I right? Do you remember the days of simple stories and simple faith? Do you remember when God simply was? For my agnostic or atheist friends: do you remember the time before disbelief?

From the beginning of time, man has been passing the cautionary tale of Adam and Eve down to the next generation, the tale of the poison fruit that tainted everything. I suspect we retell the story because there is no denying the cycle of self-poisoning. I suppose we tell the story in the hope of finding a cure to the inevitable disease. The pounding, irresistible *want* to supplant God with *self* is, in this natural state, unbreakable.

This, I suppose, is the want that wrecks everything. It is found in the careless word that ruins burgeoning faith. It is found in the lust for power that exploits the weak. It is found in the fists of the abusive, on the tongue of the perverse, in the ideological bent of racism, sexism, and classism. It is a tangled web that wraps around us all.

Lord, I feel it.

It is woven into our DNA.

Do you feel it too?

The poison defies the mechanics of time and reaches from the past, into the present, and through to the future. The smallest bit of it taints everything it touches, and that taint spreads from particle to particle until it reaches beyond the finite and into the forever.

The poison of humanity is the wellspring of death. It is bitter gall to the thirsty, stinging sweat in the eye of new faith.

It is Peter's denial of the Christ he knew. Thrice.

It is the black blood of Judas spilt over such a dark field.

All this poison spreads through the veins of humanity. It spreads sickness, pain, and atrophy. And we, poisoned children, inflict it on others. I was stung by the faith healer. I'm sure I've spread his poison to others along the way. Lord, I lament this.

It has been sixty-four days since my last drink. I am sixty-four days into the process of coming clean. With the help of a good therapist, I've walked this path of sobriety, and though it has been painful, it has been enlightening. And now here I am, at the point of decision. Will I practice the way of forgiveness? This, I think, is the antidote to the poison.

Without forgiveness, there is no meaningful way to move into healing and peace. This may sound like a conclusory and rather dogged opinion. I'll admit it. But if sobriety is to be my lot, I suppose I must find the resolution of things that quenches the fire and the desire to drown all feeling forever. In going into it, the pain, the groaning, I suppose I must be the bearer of reconciliation. Doesn't Scripture call us that, the agents of reconciliation (2 Cor. 5:18)?

It is an angst-filled prospect, but I hear the resonant voice of God: *I will never leave you nor forsake you.* I hope it is true.

NOVEMBER 26

The Spirit you received does not make you slaves,
so that you live in fear again; rather, the Spirit you
received brought about your adoption to sonship.
And by him we cry, "Abba, Father."
—ROMANS 8:15

I am a southern male, and so all of this talk about pain, frayed nerves, poisoned souls, and therapists is somewhat difficult. Acquaintances, especially my more metropolitan ones, tell me there is no reason for embarrassment, but as an over-generalization, we southern gentlemen are a bootstrapping lot. We like to believe we can lick any enemy. Yes, in the event of being snakebit, we could tie our own tourniquets, use our pocketknives to make the deep incision, and suck the wound and spit to remove the poison.

We are self-sufficient men, see.

As a result, notions of dependency are stigmatized. We like to build ladders from the ground up, erect structures for pulling ourselves from mud pits. We'd rather not resort to the help of others, much less professional help. In some respects, this is born of a genteel spirit, I reckon. Let's not burden others with our troubles and whatnot. In other respects, though, this is nothing more than foolhardy pride: I ain't broke; there's nothing to see here; move along, move along.

Even a southern gentleman can benefit from a good therapist, though, and I have come to think of mine as someone to whom I can complain without judgment. He knows I am a mired-down patient, a stuck fellow in need of a way out. He's good with tools and has provided me with a shopful of them. He reminds me that tools are useful only if used. There's a good word in there.

He sent me another tool this week, a tool to help as I push into the work of forgiveness. It is an internet link to a YouTube video, and he asked me to watch the last twenty minutes of it. It was a recording of a lecture given by Sue Johnson, a leading expert in the field of Emotionally Focused Therapy, or EFT.

"Johnson deals primarily with marriage and couples' therapy," he texted, "but I think there is something here for you."

I unwrap a sandwich from Richard's Meat Market, bite through cracked wheat, lettuce, pickle, onion, and turkey, and then I click the link. A three-dollar sandwich and a therapy video—this is not the sexiest of lunches.

I drag the time stamp to the fifty-five minute mark, and Johnson's dry British accent quips, "Effective dependency makes us stronger as individuals." This is not the salve I had anticipated, and it rubs raw against my bootstrapping heritage. She is a by-God scientist, though, and so I give her the benefit of the doubt.

Johnson describes how those who are secure in healthy, dependent attachments, those who feel safe in what she calls a bonded love, define themselves in more positive terms, are more coherent about who they are in relation to the rest of the world. Securely attached people are able to move with great freedom into spaces of forgiveness.

She turns to the Dalai Llama, describes how he holds fast to the love of his mother, how he carries it within him. It is a present, real love, one which calms him and bolsters his nonviolent stance, she says. It is so real, in fact, that he counsels his monks to carry the same love with them, to say the word *mother* when they are anxious or afraid. And now, she says, science teaches us that this not just a hokey religious practice relegated to the halls of Buddhist temples. Instead, she says, research indicates that if you "prime the attachment system by mentioning the name . . . of the people you love, [you] calm down and regulate emotions . . . [you] are more open to others.

"If you can seek comfort in the arms of another," she says, "you can handle the worst the world has to offer."

Her thesis then gets my attention: those who experience well-bonded love, she argues, are more able to forgive.

I consider this, feel the confluence of psychology and spirituality. Some might consider this some syncretistic marriage of Christianity and humanism, this combining of psychology and spirituality. I remember, though, John Michael Talbot, the Ozarkan monk who once said, "Didn't God create me with psychology?"

Prone to wander, Lord, I feel it. But this never-leaving, ever-abiding God keeps sending me back to the days of early faith—back to the garden, back to the trees. He is deconstructing every structure I ever created to keep him out. He is my bonded love.

I can go into the pain with the bonded love of an ever-abiding God. I can walk into the cave of the soul, experience the death of the death whisperers. I know this.

There is a trick to this mystery of faith, I think. It is not a difficult concept, but in practice, it's harder than charging hell with water pistols. See the God who was with you as a child. Hear him tell you he never left, not even in the darkest days. Believe him; count him as your bonded love, the two of you fused closer than bone and marrow. Follow this path of life knowing he is in you and you are in him.

This is the truth.

I know the next calling. It is to wade into the pain, to call it by name, and to forgive. I feel the flood of anxiety. *Fight or flee; fight or flee.* My amygdala is firing on all cylinders. This is the flesh's fight against spiritual actualization. The Buddhist monks cry the name of their earthly mothers in these moments of anxiety. I cry the name of love Jesus spoke in his own anxiety.

"Abba!"

Lord Jesus Christ, Son of God, have mercy on me, a sinner. Abba, have an ever-abiding mercy.

The therapist took a sip of water from his white mug, and the gentle computer tapping stopped as he looked up. "Learn to stare the accuser down," he said. "Learn to feel the sting of his words. Then learn to extend forgiveness."

There is a rub here. I am tempted to turn forgiveness into an abstract idea, to mutter, "I forgive; why not?" under my breath and continue carrying the injuries. Forgiveness is easy to feign, after all.

What's more, how do I forgive a man I do not know? The itinerant faith healer has no name in my memory, and I don't suppose I could find him if I tried. Should I call the Full Gospel church? Should I ask, "Do you recall the traveling preacher who brought his ten-pound Bible, a gallon jug of olive oil, and a mouthful of empty promises to your church back in the summer of 1984?" This, I reckon, would be a fruitless exercise.

Even more a quandary, how do you forgive a system of faith? How do you forgive those who taught you to strip God of any abiding healing power? There is no ambassador here. It is a general ghost that haunts.

It's a lesson that can be taught only by Christ. His forgiveness, his reconciliation—it's quantum. It extends both back through history and forward into our present, and through to the future. Isn't it Christ who made a way for the reconciliation of the patriarchs who were long dead before his day (Heb. 11:8–40)? Isn't it the forgiveness of Christ that reaches into the future and provides reconciliation to us, even today (1 John 3:1)? To be a forgiving people, to be the people of Christ's cross, shouldn't we go back into our own histories and extend forgiveness to those who have brought us pain, shame, and guilt?

Forgiveness is the path to spiritual wholeness, I know. But it is no easy path. And I must begin to walk it.

Lord Jesus Christ, Son of God, have mercy on me, a sinner. Teach me the meaning of forgiveness.

NOVEMBER 29

It is the weekend of Thanksgiving, and as is our tradition, we have traveled to northern Alabama to celebrate with Amber's family. I loaded up Isaac, Jude, and Ian and headed into the heart of the Bible Belt. Amber came straight from the land of the Nor-people, traveled through barren Iowa cornfields, under the St. Louis Arch, and over the Memphis bridge before arriving in her hometown. Our family has not been under the same roof for more than two weeks, and we reconvene in a sturdy brick home perched on a cliff that marks the southernmost boundary of the Appalachian foothills.

Amber comes from decent folks, members of a more conservative denomination of Christianity that does not suffer imbibers of whiskey or wine. This is a relief inasmuch as Thanksgiving dinner will not be accompanied by the libations of my more moderate family, and though I'm for moderation, it seems that, in this season, it's easier to be around the teetotaling sort.

The Carothers of northern Alabama are a good and loving lot of giants. Paul, Amber's father, is an imposing character who ducks under door frames when entering a room. Her mother is no slight woman either, she being over six feet tall. Amber's two younger brothers are as tall as their daddy, and her sister is almost six feet tall. Amber, standing at five eight, is the runt of the litter.

They are as long on opinion as they are in the leg, and from time to time our exchanges regarding politics, religion, and history generate more heat than the cast iron furnace in the living room. They are more Republican than prayer in public school, more conservative than a nun's undergarments.

I am the NPR sort; they are the Fox News Channel sort. I am more prone to see the middle ground. Often we do not see eye to eye.

The more heated political exchanges often occur as we wait for either breakfast or supper. (Perhaps it should come as no surprise that the first course of both of these meals tends to be a healthy dose of Fox News Channel viewing.) Often we find ourselves thick in disagreement there in the living room, and as things reach a respectable boil, Amber's mother will call from the kitchen, telling us it is time to eat. Shelving political banter for the time being, we gather in the neutral zone between living room and kitchen, and we hold hands in prayer.

"Forgive us our sins," Paul prays, as if recognizing that we've been teetering on the edge of some great familial divide, that we need to extend forgiveness to each other, "and we pray that you'd heal Titus." It is the humblest, quietest prayer. I can sense the stilling of spirits, the calming of emotions. We gather under the banner of Jesus' forgiveness, seeking common healing.

Titus sneaked into the guest bedroom at five thirty this morning in a droopy diaper—spindle limbs and exposed ribs—and he woke me. With hands cupped around my face, he said, "Juice, Dadda, juice." I threw my leg from the bed and swung him up with my arm in a fluid motion. He put his head on my shoulder, nuzzled into the soft spot just under my collarbone. Shirtless, I felt his bones against my ribs, and I reached and tickled his side. He jerked, laughed, and said, "Again, Dadda, again."

I missed my son while he was at the Mayo Clinic.

He had gained no weight since his visit to Mayo, and though this should not be surprising, I felt his frailty as he wriggled away from his morning tickles. I felt the heat rising in the whispers of my inner dialogue. "Where is the healing of your abiding God? Where is your faith?"

There is always a catalyst for fire, always the potential for cracking open the perforated cap of a gin bottle, for throwing the cap to the wind and crawling into a drunken bliss. This morning was an opportunity for the roots of relapse to take hold.

I opened the door to the refrigerator and reached for the juice.

"Father, you will never leave me nor forsake me." I repeated this like a mantra, and I felt the steel in my legs. I felt the regulation of emotion. I unscrewed the lid to Titus's sippy cup and prayed, "Lord, forgive my unbelief."

Forgive my unbelief. It slipped out as routine until I realized what I was asking. Such a grand request, isn't it?

The Jesus of the Gospels was a forgiving Christ. In the gospel of Luke, we see a paralytic brought to Jesus. Jesus greets him, tells him to take heart, and offers, "Your sins are forgiven." The Pharisees overhear, harbor accusations of blasphemy against Jesus, whisper among themselves. After all, what man can forgive the sins of another man? What man can restore standing between another man and God? Jesus, the Christ of X-ray vision, sees to the heart of the matter, asks the high-horsed teachers which is easier, to heal a man or forgive his sins? Then almost as an afterthought, Jesus turns to the man and says, "Get up, take your mat and go home" (Luke 5:17–26).

Christ came to restore the paralyzed man's motor skills, yes. But was this his original intent? Is the Christ of the Scriptures ever concerned with our physical maladies? Sure. But perhaps he is even more concerned with repairing spiritual breaches.

I have been such a wounded, malnourished faith-bearer. I have questioned God's presence, have questioned his ability to reach into my life. I have refused to take him into the darker caves of the soul, and this morning I felt the need for forgiveness for my utter and hopeless lack of faith.

I considered my need. I once internalized childhood pain, allowed a small wound to fester, to become gangrenous.

Lord, forgive my unbelief!

I nurtured pain like a mother nurtures her only child.

Lord, forgive my unbelief!

I constructed walls around my soul, adopted views of the Holy Spirit that did not allow for healthy conversation. I set up structures to keep God at arm's length, to keep him from taking me into the pain.

Lord, forgive my unbelief!

When the structures failed, when Titus's sickness threatened to undo life, the nerves unfurled, the fires of pain shooting through the soul door like a backdraft, like an unstoppable inferno. God could not heal; he was not enough, I thought. I shall pray no more.

Lord, forgive my unbelief!

I screwed the top to Titus's full sippy cup tight and handed it to him. He pulled it to his chest, held it tight like a prize.

Forgive my unbelief. Fill me with belief.

And that is when I heard the gentle whisper that is becoming more familiar.

"Forgiveness? Yes. But what is the nature of the forgiveness you extend toward others? What forgiveness have you extended to the faith healer?"

I heard the echo from Jesus' Sermon on the Mount.

⌒

Jesus, in his most famous sermon, stood on the mountaintop and taught the God seekers the perfect prayer. It was short, simple, and understandable even to the frailest mind and the ficklest heart. In it, he taught that we should pray, "Forgive us our sins, as we forgive those who sin against us."

As we forgive, like we forgive, in the same way we forgive—we ask you to forgive us.

If Jesus had stopped here, it would have been conviction enough for a lifetime. Jesus, though, doubled down, concluded his teaching with the *coup de grâce* of forgiveness statements: "If you forgive others their trespasses, your heavenly Father will also forgive you, but if you do not forgive others their trespasses, neither will your Father forgive your trespasses" (Matt. 6:14–15 ESV).

Each of the Synoptic Gospels contains a similar teaching. In Mark, Jesus taught, "And when you stand praying, if you hold anything against anyone, forgive them, so that your Father in heaven may forgive you your sins" (Mark 11:25). In Luke, after his teachings on mercy, Jesus preached, "Do not judge, and you will not be judged. Do not condemn, and you will not be condemned. Forgive, and you will be forgiven" (Luke 6:37).

In the eighteenth chapter of Matthew, Jesus addressed the topic of forgiveness in a parable. A king, he said, desired to settle his accounts, and brought a servant to him who owed an enormous amount. The servant pled for mercy, begged for more time so that he could pay the king back. The king listened to the groveling servant and in pity canceled the debt and sent the servant on his way. Leaving the court, the forgiven servant ran upon another, a man who owed him a much smaller amount. The forgiven servant demanded payment in full. The other had no money, pled for mercy. The king's debtor, though, showed no pity and had the man thrown into debtors' prison.

In Jesus' parable, the king hears of the wicked servant's deed and summons him to court. "Didn't I forgive you your debt?" the king asked. "Shouldn't you have had mercy on your fellow servant?" Irate, the king threw the man in prison and required that he be tortured until he paid back all that was owed.

I ask God for forgiveness of my unbelief, of my dependency on liquor, of my failure to offer penitent prayers. I ask and ask—forgive me, me, me—but how often do I consider extending forgiveness to others? Have I forgiven my fellow man for wielding theologies like blunted swords? Have I forgiven those God servants who created church structures to avoid interaction with a real and present God?

Have I forgiven myself for holding on to so much doubt, anger, and bitterness?

No.

I say I have forgiven, yet I harbor darker hatreds and cynicism. This was the most sobering realization.

A notion crept. The quality of my presence with God, the extent to which he might offer his healing, is proportionate to the extent to which I'm willing to extend forgiveness to others. I know I have a long, good work ahead of me.

Lord Jesus Christ, Son of God, have mercy on me, a sinner. Create in me a heart of forgiveness, and forgive my unbelief.

DECEMBER 1

For too long, I've carried prayer like dead weight, tossed it heavenward as if it might somehow float, only to find it crashing onto the floor, sinking into it, becoming one with the dust of nothing.

It is a lumbering thing, prayer. I imagine my prayers are like Peter walking on the water. They are filled with brash hope and promise; for all their boldness, you might think my prayers would glide over the tumultuous sea to the water-walking Christ. I pray them, though, only to find that I have faith no greater than Peter's, that my prayers are broken, that they sink into the torrent of life.

Why?

If we are an unforgiving lot, can we expect forgiveness? Can we find unity in prayer with the will of God if we do not first find unity with our fellow man?

Yes, unforgiveness breaks unity from man to man; it severs ties. In the same way, though, it is the tar that clings to our best-intentioned prayers, that turns offerings from fragrant to pungent. Unforgiveness is the measure of our disunity with God.

My prayers have been tarred-over sinking things. They have been sinking from the weight of unforgiveness. And here I am, groping for God.

There were years when my prayers felt groggy, when they danced as if to funeral dirges. There were years when I came to the table of prayer only to remember that I am a sinner and he is God, and I am always and ever under blood. "Holy is your name" was a prayable prayer. "Give us this day our daily bread" and "Bring healing" were a sucker's bets.

Why pray for the bread of healing? Why pray for the bread of direct leading? My God lived in a cessationist box, he the God who refrained more than he didn't. I supposed him a man with a set of fancy tops; he had set us all spinning in motion and walked away. He left us to bump into one another, to wobble from time to time. He left some of us to fall to the floor.

In the mesquite trees of Texas, God was not so distant. I prayed and played with a good and loving God. He was there in the wind, in the whisper. I remember him less like a concept and more like a present friend. And then, one day, I asked for a gift and he said no. I reckon I blamed him for that, even as a boy. I reckon I sowed seeds of unforgiveness that day: unforgiveness toward the faith healer for giving me false hope, unforgiveness toward myself for lacking the faith to move a minor molehill, unforgiveness toward a good God who had chosen something other than what I had asked for.

DECEMBER 2

The foul word, the fist, harmful theologies, the sexual dalliance, the pursuit of self—these are the fangs that inject the poison of bitterness, anger, and malice. The poison saturates the spirit, and without the antidote, it is too much. I chose alcohol to cope; others choose the eating disorder, the manipulation, the pornography habit, the cutting, the pills, the unbending idolatry of the intellect. And if we give a foothold to these coping mechanisms, don't they change our character? Don't we become the very thing we most despise? Don't we inject the painful poison into our own kin?

There is an antidote to this pain. Christ offered it to his enemies, his accusers, and he taught us to extend it to ours. He said, "Father, forgive them" (Luke 23:34). He entered eternity at peace with his fellow man.

We, though, cling to the wrongs wrought against us. We cuddle our pain like a newborn pup, hold to bitterness against our brothers and sisters, our mothers and fathers. We internalize it, adopt it as part of our identity. We nurture loyalty to our wounds, count it as some grand virtue of being human. Yes, we develop a fierce affection for our poison.

Unforgiveness is the ultimate act of the human will, I think. It is a private declaration that we know better than Christ, that we'd sooner our enemies receive their just deserts than find reconciliation.

Yet without forgiveness, we do not receive forgiveness. Without forgiveness, we compromise our unity with the Spirit. And without unity, where is the peace? Without peace, coping mechanisms make much more sense. Don't they?

Forgiveness is the way of God. It begins along the path through pain; it stares down the perpetrator; it releases all debts. Forgiveness is the path to peace.

Lord Jesus Christ, Son of God, have mercy on me. Teach me to forgive those I count as debtors: the faith healer, the theology wielders. Remove the poison from my life and restore my fellowship with you.

DECEMBER 3

Two nights ago, we attended a prayer meeting for Titus in Alabama. There, a shift happened, and though I've been processing it, I haven't yet committed it to my journal.

Grant is nestled in the Appalachian foothills, a place so thick with old-time religion that the car tires hum "Amazing Grace" when they roll over the highway's rumble strips. I once tried to count the roadside churches between Muscle Shoals and Grant; I lost count somewhere in the hundreds.

Those foothills are thick with God.

On Sunday evening, we drive from the top of the mountain down and into the valley of Owens Cross Roads. As we descend the ridgeline into the valley, the Alabama countryside lies exposed, the chopped corn and cotton fields barren now. The hardwoods are still finishing their autumn disrobing, and straggling leaves are burnt shades of red, purple, and yellow. Farmhouses scatter across the valley below, and smoke billows from their chimneys. I imagine them as saints offering incense after the harvest.

The elders of my in-laws' church had called Paul, asked him whether we'd carry Titus to the meeting house for a moment of special prayer. They are the good people of the Alabama valley, the good people of Owens Cross Roads, so Paul agreed.

I sit in the passenger seat on the way down the mountain, nerves fraying with every bump of the road. My palms sweat as I consider the many ways well-meaning men might put our faith on the spot.

At the church, we are ushered into a small conference room, and Amber gives a brief report. In layperson's terms, she explains that the doctors at Mayo have discovered that Titus has esophageal issues and a brain malformation. They are still not quite sure of the cause of his sickness. The preacher is a small, round man, and he wears khakis and a modest blue blazer. He listens, head nodding, hands folded over his belly. He says, "We'd like to pray for him and anoint him with oil, if that would be okay."

He reminds us that in the early church, the elders were admonished to anoint the sick with oil, to pray for healing (James 5:14). These good men of Owens Cross Roads take that admonishment to heart. They have sincere faces and their words are gentle. They are doing the best they know, but even still, my breath is starting to draw short and my forehead sweats.

The preacher reaches for a jug of oil, pours what seems like a quarter cup of it into his hand. These are kind hands, I know. And I doubt this oil is from the sale rack at the Piggly Wiggly. Even so, when we close our eyes for prayer, I am transported into the darker places. I can hear the sweet cicada song of that summer's night long ago, feel the oil cross on my forehead, feel nothing of the Spirit at work, no sensation of the miraculous variety.

I remember the faith healer, the olive oil, the promise of faith healing. There is a swirling notion that this is somehow different, but I hear the whispers from the cave of the soul: "Where is your faith, boy? Where is your God?"

I want to vomit.

But here, before the complete unwinding, I hear the gentle call of God. "I was with you in the mesquite trees; I will never leave you. I will never leave Titus."

Yes, God is in the room with us, with me, the preacher, and my Titus, whose hair and forehead are now slathered with olive oil.

My nerves begin to calm.

The preacher prays, "Lord, we do not know how or even if you will heal, but we beg you to respond. We are frail in our prayers.

Please forgive us, and forgive all our sins as we forgive others. Amen."

As we forgive others.

I think of the faith healer who attempted to barter for God's healing with a little boy's faith. I consider the lies that were injected into my young psyche, that God was neither present nor healing. His prayer was so different from that of the humble preacher at Owens Cross Roads. The faith healer was full of spiritual bravado, without regard for mystery, humility, or forgiveness. He offered up a sacrifice of a child's faith, as if the whipping up of good courage was the impetus of the miraculous hand of God. I taste the bitterness that grew in my heart over the years, the anger and cynicism toward God.

I am still holding to grudges. I need forgiveness; the faith healer does too. If the nature of God's forgiveness to me is characterized by my forgiveness to others, I reckon I am a sorry sack.

In the quiet space among the humble men at Owens Cross Roads, in these foothills thick with God, I picture this childhood moment and offer my own prayer. "Father, forgive," I pray. "Forgive the human, frail, fellow servant in that Assembly of God all those years ago." I see him in my mind with his oversized Bible and jug of oil. I hear his words: "If you have enough faith."

"It is a lie," I offer in the quieter places of my heart, "but I forgive you."

In that moment, there is a breaking. I feel it, and the fire turns to ash.

If forgiveness is a letting go, then that is what I will do.

I release him from haunting my past, my present, and my future. I have given him permission to leave the cave of my soul; I allow the light of Christ's forgiveness into the darkness.

"I thank you, God, for most this amazing day."

I pray with E. E. Cummings and look through the morning window to see snow blanketing the ground in Fayetteville. I walk to the front door in my pajamas, open the door, and stand barefoot on the cold concrete of the front porch. A winter chill is an exhilarating thing, a thing that reminds me that I am alive in the wide, wild world.

The flakes are small—spit snow, I've always called it—but they are falling fast and hard and are piling up on the ground. A white blanket stretches across the neighborhood, into the town, and out into the rural areas. It stretches onto mountains and into valleys, covers the banks of the Illinois watershed, the sides of the Boston Mountains. I imagine the view from Hawksbill, how the valleys below are filling with an iridescent beauty, how the elk are craning their necks upward in their morning calls, how their breath is swirling upward. It is sure to be the only sound in the wild Ozark valleys this morning. I imagine them as living shofars trumpeting praise to the maker of these mountains.

The new morning snow deadens the sounds of the world. I hear no cars, no dogs barking. It is a still, silent morning. The snow blows across the porch in spirited gusts, and a tiny drift covers my toes. I dust them off, the stinging of the ice setting in, and I turn back into the house.

On my way to the coffee pot, the burn of thawing toes sets in. It's a prickling heat.

I pour coffee from the pot. Pain, whether great or small, is the reminder that we are not inanimate, plastic things. We are not machines meant to go about in numb, metallic, programmed action. We are not fungible goods, items that when broken can be replaced with other unbroken items. We are meant to feel the pain of our un-thingness.

Pain is inevitable; it's the irrefutable evidence of life.

It has been seventy-five days since my last drink, and sobriety has not come without much pain and effort. There is a constant throbbing, an ever-present stinging. This is the sting of living in a mysterious world, of being broken by it, of being broken in it.

There is a salve for this, though. There is a way to make peace with the God of the past, present, and future. Accepting the mysteries of God, his decision not to heal—this is only the starting place. From there is pain and confusion and bitterness. Going through it and taking a forgiving heart with me—this is the trick.

Yes, I forgave the faith healer at my son's own anointing for healing. But if the falling into addiction is a slippery slope of a process, then forgiveness must be a process too. I am learning forgiveness is not often a single, shining event but a continual, repetitive act. A letting go, followed by another, and another. And I must learn to keep at it.

Forgiveness, both its extension and receipt, requires a lower, humble position before both God and man. Forgiveness, both its extension and receipt, is not the natural inclination of man, and I must fight for it.

It requires that I go into the past, that I relive histories again and again until I am able to release all wrongs wrought by the frail humanity of others. I know now what the therapist means when he says I must relive the pain, I must learn to master it. He means to say that I must learn to forgive it all.

The act of forgiveness, true Christ-based forgiveness, is an extension of love; it is seeing my accuser as a human, as one who acted from his own broken understanding of the world, who just did the best he knew how. Forgiveness, true godward forgiveness, is the extension of unmitigated grace, the adoption of the prayerful hope that our enemies might receive no suffering from their imputation of suffering; it is the hope that they find a better hope.

Lord, forgive me, as I forgive my enemies.

It is a simple prayer. It is not difficult, but it is hard.

It is the first week of Advent, the season of Christ's coming. Emmanuel, God with us. I repeat it this morning and consider the coming of Christ. Fully God, he came more than clothed in flesh and bone. He came, instead, unified with flesh and bone, his inextricable godness woven into tingle-toed human experience. This, I think, is the hope of hopes.

Through the garden he went, bending his will ("not my will but yours be done") to the will of God. Into the pain he went, into the crowd of men who ripped out his beard, who thorny-crowned him the low-caste king of the Jews, who scourged him, who mocked him for the blasphemy that he claimed to be both man and God. He walked straight into the heart of the pain of having his identity, the essence of who he was, attacked by men with rigid, systematic notions of God.

Defenders of the faith, of right theology, the Jewish leaders considered themselves.

Quellers of an insurrection, of uprising, the Roman guards were.

And Jesus was the middleman, the garment stretched to ripping between two peoples with very different axes to grind.

Jesus, subjected to the worst of humanity, hung, and in his last words prayed, "Father, forgive them, for they do not know what they are doing" (Luke 23:34).

He could have prayed, "Father, forgive them their sins." After all, he forgave others their sins. Had he meant, "Forgive them their

196

sins," though, he would have prayed it. Instead, the connotation seems different, gentler. Jesus recognized that they were unknowing. Instead, I wonder whether the phrase may be read with more human intuition: *Father, forgive them; they are doing the best they know how.*

Jesus, God with us, endured the worst punishment that men's black hearts could conceive. He bent his will to the mystery of suffering and walked headlong into the painful persecution of men, even men who knew not what they did. He suffered them, though he could have reached back into his Old Testament book of tricks, could have unleashed the death angel or turned them all into pillars of salt. He did not cry a mumbling word, and as he hung crucified, his parting shot to his accusers, his dying request to the Godhead, was simple. "Father, forgive them."

Lord Jesus Christ, Son of God, have mercy on me, a sinner. Unify my flesh with your Spirit so that I might extend your forgiveness.

DECEMBER 7

If you believe that Jesus was God, then wasn't he armed with the foreknowledge of his crucifixion? If you believe that Jesus was merely a good man, a revolutionary, then wasn't he savvy enough to know that every good revolutionary dies young? There can be no doubt: the foreshadowing of Jesus' death was heavy on him, and this, I think, makes his teachings on forgiveness even more poignant.

Consider the perceiving Jesus, the one who knows the hearts of the Pharisees, the men who want nothing more than to end his messianic claims. Consider the savvy Jesus, he knowing that Roman justice suffers no revolutionary, he seeing the shadowy side of Judas. His enemies are coming, coming, always coming. They are dark horses on the horizon, always. They are walking snares, people hell-bent on a lynching.

Consider Jesus armed with this knowledge. Then consider his teachings.

"But I tell you, love your enemies and pray for those who persecute you, that you may be children of your Father in heaven" (Matt. 5:44–45). As he spoke the words, was he mindful of the religious rulers who would turn him over to Roman justice? Did he release all resentment?

Consider Jesus' command to Peter that forgiveness extend not seven times "but up to seventy times seven." As he spoke to the disciple, did his mind's eye conjure an image of the Roman torturers? Was he tempted toward future revenge; did he release that too?

A good man may teach abstract principles of forgiveness and be considered good. But when a good man teaches abstract

198

principles of forgiveness, when he carries an ethos of forgiveness in the face of the most vile of persecutions, when his dying words are an actualized extension of all of his teachings on the topic, we call him great. We call him Emmanuel, God with us.

Jesus left us with teachings, yes. He left us also with a way to peace. Through Christ's Gethsemenean bending of his will, through his suffering, through the extension of forgiveness to the persecutors of his past, present, and future, we receive forgiveness in our own right. Christ's words of forgiveness were spoken from Golgotha, but they stretched across all time in space, bending the laws of physics in a holy quantum event. They stretched backward into history, setting right the wrongs that found their genesis in Eden. The words stretched into the future too, stretched to forgive the wrongs of our day. They were powerful enough to stretch to us, to forgive us of our violences, our idolatrous missteps, our sins of unknowing.

What is the essence of Christ-centered forgiveness? It is the releasing of our debtors of all past wrongs. As Buddy Wakefield, spoken-word poet, says, "Forgiveness is releasing all hope for a better past." At the same time, though, forgiveness is the manner of preparing oneself to forgive all future debts, of releasing all expectation of a pain-free future.

Forgiveness is unbounded by time and space. It operates within the fifth dimension to this dynamic marvel we call life.

There are ways around this sort of living, yes. We can avoid the pain of the past, the confrontation of any of our accusers. We can numb everything as a way to avoid exploring our histories, to avoid the necessity of mustering a forgiving spirit. Alcohol was my best anesthesia, but any addiction will do. I don't have to tell you yours.

Coping is easier for a season, isn't it?

The best medicine for the pain, though, is to extend the forgiveness of Christ.

Jesus Christ, that's a tough pill to swallow.

DECEMBER 9

It has been eighty days since my last drink.

A friend emailed me this morning, asked whether the restlessness was easing up. The restlessness is there, always there. Just under the surface, it is there. I'm an achy, longing mess of a man, there is no doubt. I feel the taint of things, greasy as they are. I feel the acute sting of the world. See how it glitters with false salves, how it offers coping mechanisms as presents?

In the Advent season, this restlessness is most acute.

It is my first Christmas season without cable television in some time. There is no spiritual or financial reason for this; we have opted to stream our entertainment from the internet. Even still, the commercialization of the Christmas season is almost unbearable. There are mailers in the mailbox, advertisements promising satisfaction from the perfect holiday gift. Social media is littered with Christmas banter too. A friend posts a Facebook coupon for a deep discount at a big-box electronics store, writes in the post, "The perfect discount for the perfect someone." It chafes at the heart. Perfection is an illusion, a glittering plastic package of false hope.

Karl Marx was wrong: it's the illusion of perfection that's the opiate of the masses.

There are so many distractions, I think. Commerce, materialism, entertainment, the endless chase of perfection—aren't these also ways to avoid the restlessness rattling in our bones? Aren't these just another way to numb? Aren't these another sleight of hand? We become entranced people, zombies longing for the stuff of earth without thought of the truest perfect—the unity of home.

Yes, materialism promises to numb the restlessness, the pain. I wish I were exempt, but I still see every liquor bottle on every wall in every restaurant. Today, I noticed them at the Vietnamese restaurant. I'd come only for the pho, but the bottles called from behind the counter like jilted lovers, batting eyelashes like Grey Goose models. Bottles, bottles everywhere, and not a drop can I drink! I am always reminded of my desire to escape the restlessness of my spirit.

The restlessness in this hard-cornered world—it will always be shut up in me to some waxing or waning degree. It was shut up in my grandfather and grandmother. My mother had her own struggles with the family energy, as do my uncles and cousins. We are anxious doers. Maybe you have this same kind of anxious, nervous energy. But I'm finding that it wanes as I submit to the bending of my will to the mysteries of my own history, to the mysteries of faith. As I walk with Emmanuel—God with me—into the cave of the soul, as I stretch into forgiveness, there is relief from the restlessness.

Perhaps this is the process my therapist calls the mastery of the pain. I'm not sure whether I've mastered anything, but I know the old ghosts have become little more than shadows of doubt these days. They are caricatures of things that once afflicted me.

These days, I'm finding a present, abiding God. And doubting Thomas as I was—*show me healing and I'll believe!*—I'm finding God to be the healer of the soul, if not the healer of my sick son.

With his help, I will learn to extend forgiveness to those in the past and to make peace with God. I will learn to forgive and forgive and forgive, and to heal.

Today, I will go back into my interior space of prayer and contemplation. This is the cave of the soul, the place meant as a refuge for God and me. I've allowed other voices to make their home in the cave, though, allowed them to invade every dark corner. I'm grateful for the light of God, able to penetrate and expose the dark corners, the light that drives the voices in the darkness away.

The desert fathers of our faith had their caves of prayer and solitude. They fled city life, holed up in desert caves and prayed. This sort of cave dwelling wasn't without its challenges, though.

Yesterday, I read of St. Anthony, one of the desert fathers who retreated to caves for prayer. It is said that in one cave, he was plagued by so many little demons (oh, those voices that sought to undo him) that his servants believed him dead and carried him out. St. Anthony was revived and demanded to go back into the cave to face the evil spirits. There he challenged the spirits to come again, and just as they returned to torment him, a bright light exploded into the cave, scattering them all. In the quiet of the cave, finally left alone, St. Anthony asked God where he was when the demons first attacked him. God replied, "I was here and watched your battle. Because you didn't give up, because you fought well, I came."

Today, as I move back into quiet contemplation, I hope to find an interior space still free of the demons that haunt.

I hope the fight is near its finish.

Today, though, I see the dark river. There is poison there. What started as a simple question born of a faith healer's misplaced word—*why didn't God heal me?*—has grown into a channel of sickness with tributaries of bitterness, doubt, anger, and apathetic resolution. I can still feel the sting of his words.

"With enough faith, all things are possible."

I consider him. Was he a misguided colaborer, a man who thought in earnest he had the gift of healing? Was he a true faith bearer, was he holding so fast to notions of a healing God that his haphazard wielding of Scripture was coupled with all the best intentions? Was he a peddler of cheap tricks for money? Was he channeling Simon's sin, asking for some Jesus juju so he could earn a buck?

These are unanswerable questions. To know the heart of a man is a privilege reserved for God.

I know now that this could be the place reserved for communion with the light of God, a place not unlike the refuges of the desert fathers. It could be a space of peace and rest just beyond the mesquite trees of my childlike faith. But here, the voice of the faith healer has returned. He's come with cohorts too. I can see the faces of those who called me while Titus was in the hospital, those who said Titus's failure to thrive was predestined before the foundation of the world for the purpose of bringing God glory. I know these men to be kindhearted, but their words still burn.

There are real things to grieve here: the loss of childhood faith, the pain that sent me packaging God in a neat cessationist box, the loss of the mesquite-grove closeness, the sense of God's abandonment. There is also the rising want for justice, for the millstone to be tied around the neck of the one who led the childlike me down the path of doubt. I feel the rhythmic, pounding want: justice, justice, justice.

In this grieving, though, things become clear. It was a setup from the beginning. There are ways to upend faith, and the adversaries of God are well practiced in the art of deception. Take a child full of faith. Introduce the question of the strength of his faith. Allow doubt to creep in. Turn him over to a religious structure; allow the structure to be substituted for God. Allow the structure to grow and grow and grow until the child believes that he might climb it to the heavens, that he might tiptoe teeter on its pinnacle and touch the face of God.

"Yes," the Spirit confirms, though with the gentleness of a mother, "you were set up."

Everyone is set up, his words echo.

"Lord Jesus Christ, Son of God," I pray, "have mercy on me, a sinner."

The ever-abiding love of the Father—this is the ultimate bonding love. It bolsters me, gives me strength to push deeper into the secret and dark places of the soul.

"I forgive my accusers, whether well-intentioned or not, whether past or present. Father, forgive them; they don't know what they are doing. So often I don't know what I'm doing. Father, forgive us all; we don't know what we're doing.

"Father, forgive the faith healer, who hung miracles on the faith of a child; he knew not what he was doing.

"Father, forgive those who promised healing to Titus contingent on our faith; they knew not what they were doing.

"Father, forgive those who said Titus's sickness is the product of your sovereign will; they knew not what they were doing.

"Father, forgive me my doubt, my angst, my lack of trust; I was doing the best I knew how."

In the face of forgiveness, all burning wanes and wanes and wanes. In the face of forgiveness, the light of God enters the cave, fills every corner, and drives the darker voices away.

These are the simplest prayers of forgiveness, but in them, I feel the Spirit speaking peace and understanding, empathy and healing. In the moment, I know it: we are all men, all ignorant colaborers here together. The faith healer, the friends of Job, the agnostics, the atheists, me—we all grope about for God, trying to make sense of his character. Some of us fancy ourselves theologians, rest in structures and our practices. Some of us float about on mystic Spirit winds. Others live in doubt or disbelief. But we are all together, bumping into each other as we try to make sense of this cosmic moment we call life. We are sometimes the abusers, sometimes the abused. But even still, we are always loved by God; we are called to love like he loves too.

And for those of us who follow the way of Christ, we are called to forgive as Christ forgave.

I forgive my accusers, the men whose words threatened my faith. To do it, I step into the heart of God; I see them for who they are: broken, misguided, groping children. I am no different, and God has loved me, has abided with me. Why should I not extend the same patience to them?

———

Forgiveness, I am learning, cannot stand as a single, once-and-for-all event. Every morning brings a fresh coffeepot, and a fresh chance to get back to this messy and necessary work.

So this morning I went into the cave. I found my accusers and grieved their words. I breathed the words, "I forgive you." I will repeat this practice in the coming days, perhaps in the coming months. I will repeat it over my accusers until the embers of bitterness, doubt, and anger are snuffed. I will repeat it over them until I see them as God sees them. I will repeat it until the cave is electrified and ever lit with pure light, until its black river runs dry, until fresh water springs from every well and I am free.

DECEMBER 11

Yesterday, my friend Jason and I drove to the hunting lease. The lease is a country expanse, a wide valley of cleared pasture, thicket, and hardwoods. It is well kept and quiet, an attractive refuge for Ozark wildlife, for the field mice and the quail, for the owl and the squirrel, for the rabbit, for the deer.

This is the season of deer culling, of thinning the herd with bow or rifle. It is the working man's sport in the Natural State, a season where Arkansans disappear into the woods, where they tap into their primitive instincts and return to the art of the hunt.

We pulled to the outskirts of a wooded valley, a blanket of snow still covering the underbrush. He tossed me a bag of corn from the back of the Jeep and grabbed one of his own, and we tromped through the snow and down a deer path.

There were deer prints in the days-old snow. Bucks, does, and yearlings, the herd all leaving their mark. The snow had been on the ground for a week, and so the daily movements of the deer are imprinted on the hillside. Every morning, after drinking at the stream to the southeast of the wood, the deer come up the embankment and skirt the forest. They walk to the north for almost one hundred yards and turn back to the west for less than a stone's throw. They circle back to the south and pause at a sort of deer crossroads.

We are standing at the deer crossroads.

"Here," he says, and splits open his bag of corn. He pours it on the ground in a long line, and I follow suit. Over his right shoulder, I see the deer stand. This is his ambush spot.

"I try to pour the corn in a long line, hoping that it turns the

206

deer broadside to my stand." Jason is a man of calculated words, and even in his hunting he is a strategic fellow. "From here," he says, "it's about a twenty-yard shot."

I look at the expanse of wood. It is a wide area with room to roam, but even still, the deer tracks for the most part follow the same lines. They are creatures of telltale habit. They are predictable to a fault, to the death.

There are buzzards in the trees. They were circling over the fields this morning, they with their wide wings and rounded tails circling over some dead or dying creature. I don't see them now, but I can feel their beady black eyes hiding behind the branches. The buzzards stay hidden in the places of death; they are always looking for scraps of a kill.

We finish pouring the corn and walk back to the Jeep along the deer path. There are coyote tracks mixed with the deer tracks. Something else has been hunting this herd. Another pack has been looking to pick off a sick, wounded, or dying doe.

The hunter, the buzzard, the coyote—each is a different kind of predator; each, though, follows the predictable movements of the unsuspecting deer. The herd is oblivious to their stalking. They will stop and eat the corn one evening, consider it a great gift from the heavens before one of their members feels the sting of the broadhead arrow tip.

The crossroads, the corn, the tree stand, this place in the wood—it is all a setup.

It would be fool's folly to believe ourselves any less predictable than the deer. It is primal instinct, the survival mechanism that bends us toward the same paths as those before us. We walk the well-worn path, are hunted in our own right. For thousands of years, we've wandered into this human experiment all doe-eyed, only to be ambushed. And if we survive the attack, we so often return to the place of our wounding, relive the trauma, allow it to traumatize us again and again.

Jesus teaches us a different way. Well acquainted with his accusers, he did not shirk the pain or limp away. Instead, he blazed a trail into the heart of persecution, stared down death meted out at the hands of his own creation, and at his ultimate end, he extended forgiveness.

This is the way of love.

For the last several days, I have been practicing the way of Jesus. In my morning meditations, I've followed him into the pains of my history. Here I've written of the faith healer, of the well-meaning pious, of those who've used theologies like too many swords. There are others too—perhaps family members, friends, and colleagues. I've been sitting in my morning chair; I've been retracing my steps back through the pain until I find arrows. There I've stopped and spoken forgiveness over the person.

Though I suppose this could be done in the recesses of the heart, I have chosen to speak forgiveness aloud. "Father, Father, Father—I forgive the faith healer, whose unwise words robbed me of childlike faith," I've said. Perhaps it's laughable, speaking words to the wind this way, but I find that hearing my own pronouncement of forgiveness does something for my heart. I speak the words, and I feel the release of pain. I speak the words, and I feel the hope of a freer life.

Less wary of the trees these days, I've waded back through the snow and into the place of my ambush. I have practiced love in the way of forgiveness, and I'm finding myself less thirsty for coping mechanisms. I'm finding myself less in need of the liquor that numbed me up, that led me stumbling only and ever into death.

Titus walks into the room this morning, ribs exposed. He is still not gaining weight. He crawls into my lap and asks me to fill his juice cup. He is a snuggling, good-natured child who is still unaware of his sickness.

Last night, he lay in his bed and called out like only a two-year-old can: "Jesus! Jesus! You there, Jesus?" Maybe he hears things I can't. Maybe children better understand the nature of an abiding God.

At only two, Titus is finding the way to his own mesquite trees.

Will Titus receive healing? I don't know. But this I know: he is calling out to Jesus in his sickness. I can't protect him from the disappointment of an abiding sickness; I can't protect his Ozark maple grove. I can't insure his childlike faith will not be unwound. But I can show him a better way than the path I chose for myself.

I'm pressing deeper into the way of Jesus, and I feel a healing coming. This one, though, is mine.

*Forgiveness is the name of love practiced among
people who love poorly. The hard truth is that
all people love poorly. We need to forgive and be
forgiven every day, every hour increasingly. That
is the great work of love among the fellowship of
the weak that is the human family.*

—HENRI NOUWEN

The capitalist, corporate Christ was at the big-box retail store yesterday. I saw him there, a plump little Caucasian baby in a happy little inflatable crèche somewhere between the garden section and the ammo aisle. It seemed an ironic placement, the tableau of the holy birth there in the middle of both the peaceful and violent material wants of men.

I contemplated the words of Benedictine nun Sister Joan Chittister: "Christmas is really not the acme of the liturgical year. Christmas simply commemorates, not celebrates, the historical birth of Jesus, whenever that might have been. Because of Christmas, the life of Jesus was possible. Because of Christmas, the incarnation can be fulfilled at Easter. Because of Christmas, the humanity of Jesus is fact."

The humanity of Jesus is fact, just as the inflatable crèche is fact. God became flesh and dwelt among us in our meager, misguided, poor, pallid, violent, vindictive, leprous lameness. He was born to bring us a better way than the poison we choose for ourselves, to bring us healing and health. Christmas was the genesis of Christ's journey through the pain and into the reconciliatory work of Easter's rescue.

The capitalist, corporate Christ was at the big-box retail store yesterday. Though maybe there is wisdom in that scene of absurdity. Maybe, somehow, Jesus hides in the middle of it all, waiting to be discovered by the men who are pushing their way, best they know how, from the garden aisle to the gun counter, from Eden to all the world's violence. Maybe he waits for us to discover him there, to point to him in the crowds, and to say, "There is the better way."

Maybe?

The glittered star atop our Christmas tree reflects the tiny white lights strung through the tree's branches. It is the star of hope. It is Advent, and we're coming closer and closer to the manger. I see the star, the ornament of the three ships sailing, coming. We're coming closer and closer to the consummation of the season, the day when the world received the gift of "life to the full," the day we received our path to recovery. I'm trying to set my mind on it.

Christmas.

It marks the implanting of God himself in the womb of woman, the process of his becoming created and growing into manhood, into full brotherhood with the created. It is about his choosing to share in our groanings, our joys too. It is about the beginning of the Christ journey through the pain and into forgiveness, through death and into reconciliation, through sanctification and into glorification.

Christmas marks the coming of Emmanuel, God with us, God our brother.

God our brother.

I see Jesus in a great room teaching a crowd when a congregant tells him, "Your mother and brothers are standing outside, wanting to see you." Jesus surveys the push of humanity and replies, "My mother and brothers are those who hear God's word and put it into practice" (Luke 8:21). And if he had only said the words, it might have been enough. He did not stop there, though. He was born to practice his own teachings; he was born to walk the road through the pain, to the cross, and into the ultimate act of forgiveness and reconciliation. His brothers follow his path.

Some of my accusers are easier to identify than others. There are some who hide in cave shadows, though, and as I bring light deeper into the reaches of the cave, I can hear their voices too. I'll not journal about those voices here. I'm approaching ninety days of sobriety, and I think it is time to draw this journal to a close. There are acts of forgiveness that will, as sure as the rising Ozark morning, take another ninety days to unpack, and I think that's for a different journal.

I'm pressing deeper into the work of forgiving all of these voices, though. And in that work, I'm finding unity with Emmanuel, the ever-abiding God with us. I'm finding a kindred connection with Jesus, my brother. I'm finding that the simple but difficult act of forgiveness is sucking the poison from my blood; it's quenching my thirst for human salves.

This is an act of obedience, yes. It is also an act of drawing deeper into brotherhood with Christ. I consider this and whisper aloud, "Father, forgive the faith healer who stole my faith; reconcile him to you, wherever he may be." I consider the slick-haired preacher. The memory that once conjured a sense of abandonment now brings a reminder of brotherhood. The man whose words once bore only anxiety now brings an opportunity to be brothers with Christ.

When we practice forgiveness, when we extend love to our accusers, we are choosing to allow our histories to be rewritten;

we are choosing to allow those things that once brought only pain to bring us a sense of unity with Christ. When we practice forgiveness, we take on the mantle of Jesus' kin. We allow him to claim us as brother. This is a grand opportunity. Perhaps, this is the greatest Christmas present.

I began this journal as a ninety-day exposition of coming clean. I see it now, the arc that rises in a crescendo and falls toward resolution. This is the story of moving from doubt to belief, from drunk to sober, from prodigal to unified with the Christ of my youth, the Christ in the mesquite trees. I have heard the still small voice, followed it into the cave of the soul, where my unforgiven accusers lay in wait. In the end, I found that embodying Christ's forgiveness drives these voices from the cave and brings peace to the interior life.

I suppose it really was a setup after all.

Yes, this started as a journal with no arc, but here we are in the beginning of resolution. I'll say beginning because I don't want to jinx it. (I know it won't be all resolved until death releases us from this present reality.) Is there a message locked inside me? Yes. Scripture teaches that a disciple is not above his teacher, but everyone, when he is fully trained, will be like his teacher (Luke 6:40). How then should we live?

Father, forgive them; they don't know what they are doing.

———

We are an odd company, this family we call the church. I don't suppose I'm special among you, that I'm the only one who confesses the power of a risen Christ on Sunday morning and drinks himself into the icy numbness. I don't suppose I'm the only one who hoards hurts until well after the accusers have disappeared or passed on. I don't suppose I'm the only one who has let the perception that God is dormant burn and burn.

You know this pain, yes? For some, perhaps it's the itinerant preacher, but for others, maybe it's the runaway father, the dead mother, or the friend who's disappeared. For some it's a minor pain that's allowed to fester—mine was—but for others it's the unfathomable, unthinkable pain of abuse, rape, prejudice, or murder.

You feel it, don't you? They are still there, your accusers, and they are hurling accusations, aren't they? They are still in your caves, in your ears, in your veins, yes? You taste them, smell them.

Has it upended your faith in God, in yourself? Has it driven you to self-soothing, to the icy numbness of sex or materialism or even theology? Has it created in you an agnostic heart, an agoraphobic heart, an alcoholic heart?

Perhaps this is all too mystical for you; perhaps you are uncomfortable with the simplicity of a Jesus who abides with the simplest faith-bearers—with the children and the forgivers. Maybe you'd rather find comfort in the cold adult numbness, the coping mechanisms: the booze, the sex, the chocolate, the systematized theologies that reduce God to a proper but cold equation. Maybe you'd rather build structures around your pain, tuck them behind protected and thorny hedgerows, hold them in a safe place of your making.

But I see through your drinking, your affair, your theological systems. I know all addiction is undergirded with pain, and when you strip the addiction away, all questions, doubts, and accusations are sure to come screaming to the surface.

Be honest: in moments of clarity, of stone-cold sobriety, do you ask how a good God could allow so much pain? Do you wonder whether Jesus is a figment of your imagination, whether God is real? Do you have fond dreams of dying—not of suicide but of dying? Do you see the prospect of death as release? Do you lust after money and power so much that you poor yourself down and skinny yourself up to try to assuage that guilt? Do you have so much money and power that it scares you, that you wonder whether you are the rich man who'll sooner be screwed than enter the eye of the needle? Perhaps you love your spouse, perhaps you don't, but do you love yourself and do you forgive yourself the way God loves and forgives you? Do you wonder whether God will ever speak again, and whether he ever spoke in the first place? Do you wonder whether it's just your noggin talking to you? Do you wonder whether God likes you? Do you hear your accusers casting aspersions, telling you that you're unloved, unworthy, a thing to be discarded?

I know you ask these questions, that you hear these accusations and feel the pain. How do I know this? You are my brothers and sisters. We're all human, aren't we? We're all more alike than we'd like to admit, we sinner-saints.

Perhaps there are many of us who need to move from a place of addiction (any old addiction) to freedom. The process hurts, there is no doubt, and I know I'm not yet done. There is more guano in the cave to wade through, and sure as shooting, the bats will keep dropping it. There's more pain to explore and more accusers to forgive. It's going to hurt, there's no doubt. But if we are going to practice the forgiveness taught by Jesus, if we are going to find the freedom of reconciliation with our enemies, and in that find reconciliation with God, perhaps it's time for a serious exploration of our pains and anxieties. Perhaps it's time to leave those behind in favor of an abiding God, a God who never leaves, never forsakes. Perhaps it's time for our own coming clean.

I remember the days in the mesquite trees. Those were the good days when I felt the presence of God, before the meddling of men, before their dim theologies stripped me of childlike joy. This morning, I hear God again. He's here, reminding me that he never left, but it was my cynicism, my unforgiveness, my stubborn will and pious systems that drowned the gentle whisper.

Remember.

I told you this isn't a clean story. It does not move through conflict to perfect and complete resolution. Instead, it moves to a simpler end: God is mystery. His Spirit speaks to babes and children, and if we let it, it'll speak to us still. It will speak first, "Forgive," and then, who knows? The Spirit is like a wind, you know.

DECEMBER 19

I woke this morning to my ninetieth day of sobriety. It is a day that I wish were marked by the morning melody of the robin or the cardinal—the staple songbirds of the Ozarks—but they've all flown the coop for the winter. Outside there is only a soft wind and the quiet cold.

I light the Christmas tree in the corner of the room, watch the star of promise reflecting again. For unto us a child was born, is being born, will be born again! He is Emmanuel, God with us, and he came to walk as humans walk; he came to show us the path to peace. Thirty-six years into life, and I wonder whether I've finally found him, whether I've finally found his road by being born into a forgiving heart.

I peek through the door to Titus's room, and he is lying with Jude on the bottom bunk. They are asleep to the world—its prospective pains and joys alike—and their faces are free of care. Titus has stripped his shirt off in the night, and I see his exposed ribs. He is still rail thin and gaunt, still without healing. He is making it through, though, and each day his eyes grow a little brighter, shining like the coming Christmas star. By his sickness, I have been drawn closer to the Christ who was swaddled in the manger— Emmanuel, God with us.

Sobriety has become second nature these days. Though on occasion, the thirst for whiskey or gin comes calling. On occasion, the pit of my stomach leaps at the thought of supple red wine. I don't suspect this will stop anytime soon. Life will do what life does, and some stressor will rear its head. This world is quite adept at triggering pain. I'll be tempted to allow the mocking voices back into the cave of my soul, back into the place reserved for communion with God, but I hope I'll remember the way of inner sobriety. It's the way of bending my will to the mystery of God, of facing pain, of forgiving those who've inflicted wounds and will inflict wounds in the future.

Yes, this is the way of our Christ.

There is a powerful peace in the reconciliation of Christ. There is peace for the taking, and peace for the making. There is an end to the mocking voices. There is a quantum reckoning. I know. My Lord told me so.

"Peace I leave with you; my peace I give to you. Not as the world gives do I give to you. Let not your hearts be troubled, neither let them be afraid. . . . Rise, let us go from here" (John 14:27–31 ESV).

AFTERWORD
A Word on Titus

It has been almost a year and a half since I wrote the journal
that became *Coming Clean*, and Titus is still a thin child. That
being said, after the last entry, the doctors prescribed medication
for his esophageal issue, which seems to be working. He has taken
to growing, slowly but surely. As of this update, Titus is still not
on the growth chart, but he is well-developed cognitively and has
more energy than a wild stallion. He is a delight.

I suppose Titus could grow into a behemoth of a man. After all,
Amber's side of the family is long in the leg, and Titus's genes could
kick in at some point. But part of living, I suppose, is releasing
expectations for your children. I don't expect Titus to be anything
other than what Titus will be. And if you could meet him, if you
could play tag with him in the back yard or draw with him at the
dining room table, you'd know that if there is any word to describe
him, it's this: miraculous.

ACKNOWLEDGMENTS

Amber: from the moment of my first confession of addiction, you embodied patient love and gave me space to process the journey. You gave me more grace than I deserved and asked fewer questions than I expected. I cannot imagine sobriety without you.

Isaac, Jude, Ian, and Titus: thank you for asking me the tough questions about addiction, for asking me whether I've started drinking again when I'm cross or short. I haven't. Sobriety is a gift to me, and I hope it's one I pass on to you.

Heather: you are my sister. Thank you for being a prophetess.

Mike: shall we gather in the collective? Thank you for making space for Eucharist.

John Ray: there's blood and then there's kin; you are kin. Thank you for teaching me to be unafraid of the right questions.

Ryan: if there's a better therapist, I don't know him. Thanks for your work.

Bill: *Coming Clean* would not have been born without your gentle coaxing. Thank you for pulling it out of me. In another lifetime, you could have been a used car salesman. In this one, I'm glad you are my agent, minister, and friend.

Sobriety—from any addiction—isn't a thing worked out in solitary confinement. Instead, it comes from good and right accountability, from a community that promises to ask tough questions, expecting only honest answers. I have the best communities. Thank you, Troy, Chad, and Preston, for being my cohorts, but thank you more for being my friends. To the crew at 1900 David, thank you for sharing a roof and bearing witness to my confession; you are good people. (I don't care what they say!) To the men of the Genesis Project, you'll never know how much the invitation to the table strengthened my resolve. To the Tuscany crew, thank you for breaking bread with me in the tender days of sobriety; thank you for praying the words wounded healer over me. Joseph and Lindsey, you are my people, and I am yours. (Raclette soon?) Bramlett, why you've stuck with me I'll never know; thanks for being a big brother. Nish, Sarah, and Preston, thank you for reading my roughest drafts, but thank you more for speaking blessing over my life.

Mom: thanks for gifting me with words to process. Dad: thanks for gifting me with steadfast resolve. Schell and Paul: thanks for sharing your home during all those doctor's visits to Little Rock; more, thank you for your toffee.

Stephanie: you caught the vision of *Coming Clean* when it was in its infancy, when I was still shaky on the sharing. For that I will be forever grateful. This project would not have seen the light of day without your enthusiasm, attentiveness, and skill.

Finally, to the team at Zondervan: you are a gift.